From the bottom of heart. Thank y
for supporting and buying my book.
I hope you enjoy it as much as
i enjoyed writting. Best wishes
in your advance in the wine world.
The more you will learn
the more you will fall in
love with the wine world.

Dennis A. Cruz
D. Lobo Wines....

For the Love of Wine: Study guide for sommeliers and wine enthusiasts

The French Edition

References:

The Court of Master Sommeliers

GuildSomm

The Wine Cellar Insider

Wine-Searcher

Wine & Spirit Education Trust

Published by Gatekeeper Press

2167 Stringtown Rd, Suite 109

Columbus, OH 43123-2989

www.GatekeeperPress.com

ISBN (hardcover): 9781662908422

ISBN (paperback): 9781662908439

eISBN: 9781662908521

COMING SOON...

For the Love of Wine
The Italian edition

FRANCE

... BEFORE FRANCE

Introduction

Possibly dating to over 20 million years ago, winemaking seems to have been comforting us, humans, and pleasing our tastebuds since the beginning of times... When ancient Greece reached its apex, along with the birth of Dionysus, finally helped wine become the influential nectar we know of today.

Some archeologists have reported that the earliest concrete example of exhaustive vinification, however, finds its roots in the Areni-1 cave in Armenia, and dates back to around 6,100 years ago. Others have unearthed 8,000 year old Neolithic pottery fragments of wine jars, in the country of Georgia.

Entrance of Areni 1

Without a doubt, wine has a long history that is yet to be unveiled. Its current high-standing and luxurious value, however, can very easily be traced back to one small area of the world in particular: the beautiful country of France and its surprinsingly versatile landscapes and climates. That is what this book is about, and we truly hope - for the love of wine - to make you dream, travel, and want to know everything about wine and its humble origins.

Dennis Conger

Author, passionate sommelier and founder of D.Lobo Wines

Bacchus (Roman mythology)/Dionysus

Neolithic wine jars

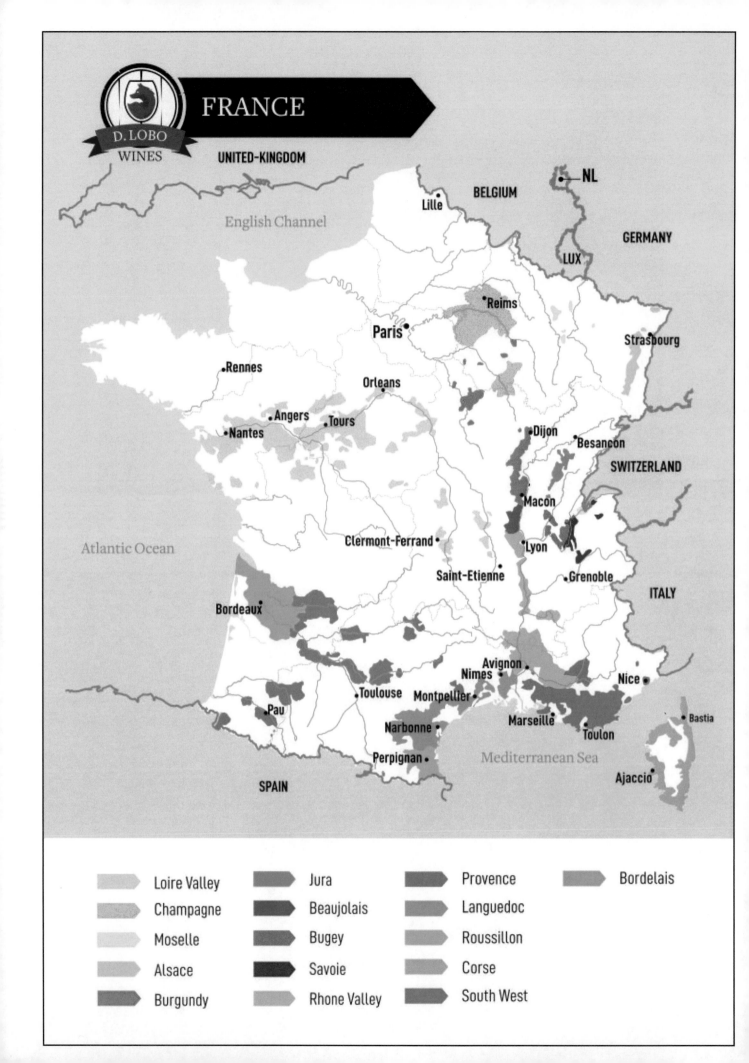

THE HISTORY OF FRENCH WINE LAW

Appellation d'Origine Protégée (AOP)

The European Union got inspired by the AOC classification's system and enacted, in 2009, the Appellation d'Origine Protégée (AOP), or protected designation of origin. This system enforces EU-wide quality standards for wine production, and has achieved and maintained excellency in the field across all EU member countries.

After the AOP system was established, two quality categories emerged:

- Wines with geographic indication
- Wines without geographic indication

In 1953, the French Institut National de l'Origine de la Qualité (INAO) inaugurated the Appellation d'Origine Contrôlée (AOC), a classification system that aims to guarantee authenticity of origin and style. This appellation quickly rose as a standard for all other member countries of the European Union.

AOC/AOP Quality Levels

Wines without geographic indication

Vin de France – 20% of all French wines

Since higher yields are permitted and no specific location of origin is required to appear on the label of a Vin de France bottle, this desgnation is known to be the most lenient. The words "Variety/Vintage" may be printed on the ephitet, and oak chips are permitted.

Wines with geographic indication

IGP (Indications Géographiques Protégées) /Vin de Pays – 30% of all French wines

This label represents 74 delimited regions, which are each divided into regional areas, departments and other types of zones. IGP enforces fewer restrictions than the AOC and AOP labels. In fact, hybrids are permitted, and bottles can be varietally labeled. Moreover, only 85% of the fruit contained in the bottle must come from the geographic region indicated on the label.

AOC/AOP – 50% of all French wines

This is the highest-esteemed and strictest designation for French wines. Indeed, all geographical boundaries under this label are precisely defined and regulated, often based on soil composition. These specific zones can represent larger regional areas, small towns, or even single vineyards. Grape varieties and viticulture methods are rigorously regulated as well, as the AOC/AOP labels define where the vines must be planted, the yield per hectare, the type of vine training used, irrigation, the minimum and maximum degrees of alcohol, aging requirements and residual sugar allowance all represent important criteria that fall under meticulous rules. Lastly, 100% of grapes must come from stated AOC/AOP designation.

A GLANCE AT BURGUNDY

Historical background

Behind each delectable glass of wine is a fascinating piece of history, just waiting to be taught and told... And your glass of Burgundy's is no exception. With this first chapter, we hope to make you travel through centuries of wine growing, making and selling in the beautiful region of Bourgogne, France.

Archaeological evidence of Burgundy's viticulture takes us all the way back to the late 1st century, an epoch marked by the bold Roman conquest of Gaul. Then, 300 years later, as the powerful Western Roman Empire collapsed, the first Burgundians-Germanic tribesmen made their glorious entrance and in turn embraced the Art and Science of winemaking. Yet, old Europe inevitably plummeted into dark ages after the fall of Rome... Which left a door open for the Catholic church, and more specifically its Benedictine order, to bloom as an influential politico-cultural force and to rise as the emblematic pioneer of vinification that we know of.

During the 10th and 11th centuries, the Benedictines and their monastery, the Cluny Abbey, temporarily "took the crown" to mature into the political and cultural center of Western-Europe and resolutely promote vine-growing among their impressive network of priories. The Cistercians – another Catholic order that sprung up from the Benedictines in the 1100's – then acquired a myriad of vineyards all across Burgundy, such as prominent Grand Cru Clos de Vougeot. The Côte d'Or's greatest vineyards, for instance, were all converted to viticulture by the 14th century. To this day, wine makers and enthusiasts owe a great deal to Cistercian and Benedictine monks, who worked tirelessly among the vines for hundreds of years and therefore played a consequential, pivotal part in the origins of Burgundy's terroir.

Without surprise, Burgundy's enticing wines ultimately emerged as a symbol of refinement and sumptuous living, making them one of Western-Europe's most expensive exports.

The Valois Dynasty and its Dukes - who ruled the region with near autonomy from 1363 until the French Crown took over in 1477 – quickly became aware of the wines' prestige and made capital out of Burgundy's ruby-tainted gold by enforcing their own quality control procedures. Indeed, while Philip the Bold instructed growers to tear off Gamay grapes in favor of lower yielding and renowned Pinot Noir's, Philip the Good would advocate for innovative hillside viticulture.

Into the bargain, Bourgogne's winemaking history cannot be told without mentioning the Hôtel-Dieu of Beaune. Founded by Valois Court nobleman Nicolas Rolin in 1443, this philanthropic hospital is one of the world's unrivaled, historic charitable institutions. In fact, it provided well-needed free care to the poor and infirm in a plague-ridden era, and over the years became the beneficiary of many donated vineyards in and around the city of Beaune (also known as the wine capital of Burgundy). Today, the Hospices de Beaune – its Domaine being one of the largest vineyard owners in the Côte de Beaune - holds an annual wine auction, with proceeds still benefitting the sick.

Until the French Revolution arose and drastically reformed the country's politics and social classes, some monastery-owned vineyards fell, in due course, into the hands of private proprietors, while others remained under clerical management. Eventually, lands owned by

bourgeoisie and churchmen alike were seized and auctioned off in the early 1790's, as a consequence of the storied uprising. Then clocked in French Emperor Napoleon who, in 1804, issued his infamous Napoleonic Code, requiring inheritances to be split equally among heirs and significantly fragmenting vineyard ownership. The impact of this decree can still be witnessed through Burgundy's current holding pattern, as present-day vineyards resemble a true patchwork... For instance, the Grand Cru Clos Vougeot alone claims over 80 different cultivators. Having less crops to work with, growers had to rely on wine merchants – négociants - to finesse the marketing and the production costs of vinification.

Until the 1920's, when Domaines gained the right to bottle the wines they produced – also known as Domaine bottling – négociants were entirely controlling Burgundy's wine sales. Appearing for the first time in the early 1700's, négociant houses were known to capitalize upon this unfortunate fracture of ownership. They would buy disparate barrels of grapes or wine, combine them and create a commercially viable product. As for winegrowers, they were generally bourgeoisie who leased the land in turn to farmers in either "metayage" (sharecropping) or "fermage" (leasing) arrangements.

Location and geography

Burgundy is located in the Eastern-Central part of France and shares a border with Switzerland. The prominent wine region is divided into five areas, listed here from north to south:

- **Chablis**
- **Côte d'Or**
    - **Côte de Nuits**
    - **Côte de Beaune**
- **Côte Chalonnaise**
- **Mâconnais**
- **Beaujolais**

Landmark: Roche de Solutré

The prehistoric Roche de Solutré is an impressive limestone hill and is the emblem of South Burgundy that is about 50,000 years old. Visitors can walk up the 500 meter high rock to enjoy a breathtaking panorama of the Mâconnais vineyards, a view that points all the way to the Alps... At the Roche's foot lies the Crot-du-Charnier deposit, which is composed of thousands of hors bones, flints and engraved stones.

Chablis

About 130 kilometers (80 miles) northwest of Dijon in the Yonne department stands the medieval municipality of Chablis, surrounded by an abundant assortment of vineyards. Other traditional wine growing townships such as Irancy, which produces Pinot Noir, Joigny, which produces Pinot Gris and Tonnerre and Vézelayn which produce Chardonnay, can be found near the better-known commune. Together, these areas are informally named "Grand Auxerrois", as they are part of the land adjoining Auxerre, capital of Yonne.

Côte d'Or

Also known as "Burgundy's Golden Slopes", the historic Côte d'Or department shelters the region's most fancy, coveted wines. Its graceful vineyards plots form a near perfect, slim bandeau that stretches for an impressive 60 kilometers (37 miles), from Dijon's outskirts and southbound through the three communes clustered around the Maranges vineyards. Dijon, as an aside, is Burgundy's official regional capital, but Beaune stands as the Côte d'Or's commercial hub for wine trade.

Branched into two northern and southern subregions - Côte de Nuits and Côte de Beaune - the "Golden Slopes" offer a spectacular landscape with its miles of lush vineyards, facing sharp timbered limestone hills. Averaging a width of 1 kilometer, the winegrowing trail grows even thinner between the towns of Corgoloin and Ladoix-Serrigny, where the dividing line between the Côtes de Nuits and de Beaune prevails.

Côte Chalonnaise

Named after the notable city of Chalon-sur-Saône, the Côte Chalonnaise lies right below the Côte d'Or, in the north of the Saône-et-Loire department. Located on the western end of the Saône River Valley, the Côte Chalonnaise's vineyards rest on a streak of divided and only slightly sloping escarpment, unlike its bordering "Golden Slopes" which primarily follows the curve of one cliff. Withal, the Saône River glides for about 60 kilometers (37 miles), from Chalon-sur-Saône to our very next interest, Mâcon...

Mâcon

The wine city of Mâcon is the capital of Saône-et-Loire and evidently the namesake of the Mâconnais's winegrowing region. Second only to the region of Chablis, the Mâconnais is one of Burgundy's largest white wine production areas, which looks a lot like its northern neighbor, the Côte Chalonnaise. The Mâconnais's landscape does however take on a more monumental face as we approach the south of the area, where sharp, rugged limestone boldly surges from their flatter surroundings. In fact, the towering limestone Rock of Solutré is one of the most emblematic touristic attractions in the department, for it is simply breathtaking.

Beaujolais

Following the jagged pattern of the Mâconnais, the Beaujolais region forms a chain of low and choppy mountains that rise as high as 1,000 meters (3,280 feet) in elevation. Named after the commune of Beaujeu, the Beaujolais area is technically located in the Rhône department but historically belongs to Burgundy. Admittedly, Beaujolais's southernmost wine-growing villages are only minutes away from Lyon and closer to Vienne's vineyards, in the Northern Rhône Valley, than to the Côte d'Or's. While its best sweet, berry flavored wines are produced on elevated northern slopes and villages, a third of the Beaujolais's winemaking takes place on its flat and vast southern land.

Burgundy's modern AOP system

The standard regional designation for the Burgundy winegrowing region is "Bourgogne AOP". Usually composed of Pinot Noir and Chardonnay grapes, Burgundy's red, white and rosé wines are all classified under that same appellation, and more bottles now eminently state the grape variety on their labels. Lesser Bourgogne varieties like Pinot Gris, Pinot Blanc and César, for instance, are sometimes included on the label but are generally limited to runner-up and tend to be withdrawn from newer vineyards. The same goes for cheaper, higher yielding Gamay grapes which - although permitted on the labels of Bourgogne AOP wines in the area of Beaujolais - were disqualified from most Bourgogne AOP rouge and rosé wines circa 2011. In the same year, wine quality authorities revitalized and rebranded the Bourgogne Grand Ordinaire AOP with a new and more contrasting appellation: Coteaux-Bourguignons AOP. Unlike Bourgogne AOP, that designation approves the inclusion of Gamay grapes in red blends and encompasses inexpensive blended white and rosé wines.

While Bourgogne AOP wines may theoretically contain grapes harvested anywhere in Burgundy, from historic Chablis to the Côte Chalonnaise, including Puligny-Montrachet or the prominent Mâconnais region, many bottles indicate more limited areas of production on their labels. In addition, certain villages, vineyards or other winegrowing regions may legally append their names to the Bourgogne AOP appellation as a way to precisely define the origin of their product. Technically, these are only "geographical designations" of the Bourgogne AOP rather than distinct appellations, but towns like Le Chapitre, La Chappelle, Chitry, Côte Saint-Jacques, Épineuil, Notre-Dame, Montrecul and Vézelay may label their wines with Bourgogne AOPs geographic classifications.

On another note, we have the Bourgogne Aligoté AOP, which is a separate designation for varietal wines that are solely composed of the white Aligoté grape. Simple, refreshing and citrusy, wines from that appellation often exhibit a surprising, palatable acidity. The Aligoté wine is usually consumed as an aperitif, or lightly blended with a sweet, generous drop of Crème de Cassis as the classic base for a flavorful Kir cocktail.

Contrastingly, some red and rosé wines are produced all across the Côte d'Or as well as in southern Burgundy, and are labeled as Bourgogne-Passe-Tout-Grains AOP. A minimum of 30% of those wines, together with 15% of their blend, are composed of Pinot Noir and Gamay grapes. Those two varieties must be vinified together in order to secure that appellation.

The Bourgogne AOP classification also covers two of the region's sparkling wines: the white Crémant de Bourgogne and the red Bourgogne Mousseux. The latter represents an older, rarer appellation that is exclusive to traditionally produced sparkling reds.

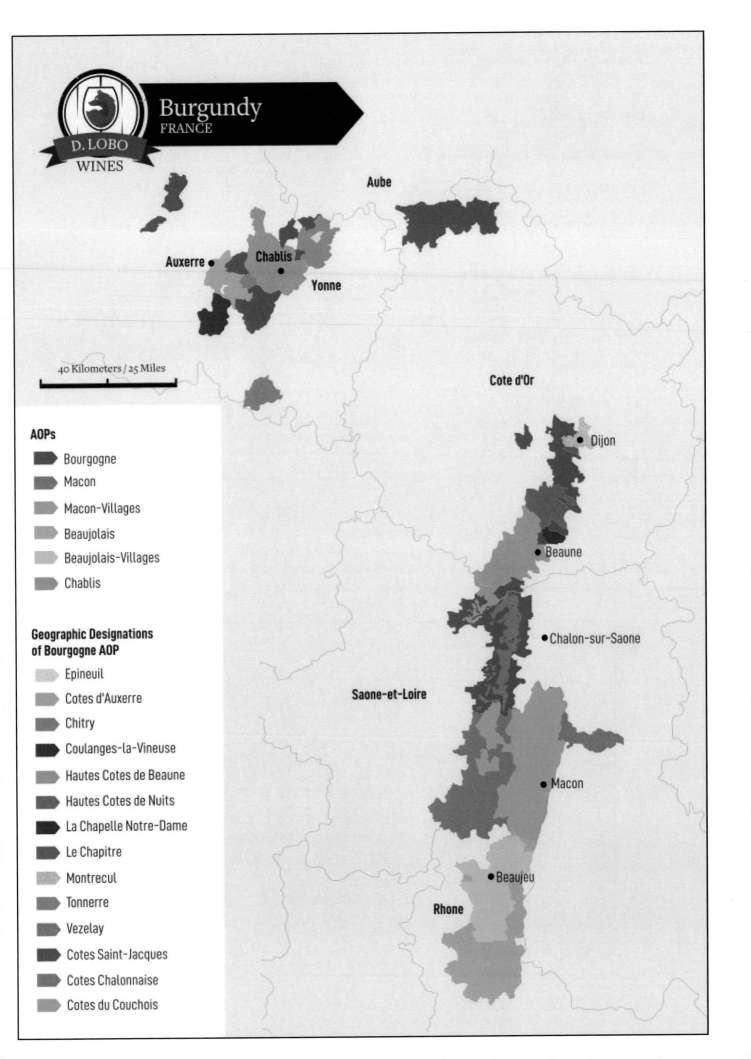

Climate

Burgundy's climate is continental.

Topography and aspects

The region displays impressive hills. Known to host the best vineyards, the Côte d'Or slope faces East and Southeast.

Soil composition

Burgundy's soils are composed of limestone, clay, chalk and marl. Beaujolais' soils, more specifically, hosts a lot of granite.

Grape varieties

White
- Chardonnay (main variety)
- Aligoté (small plots)

Red
- Pinot Noir (main variety)
- Gamay (grown primarily in Beaujolais)

Labeling law and wine Classification system

Burgundy's wine labeling system is based on specific and regulated vineyard location. As the area gets smaller, quantity decreases and quality may decrease as well.

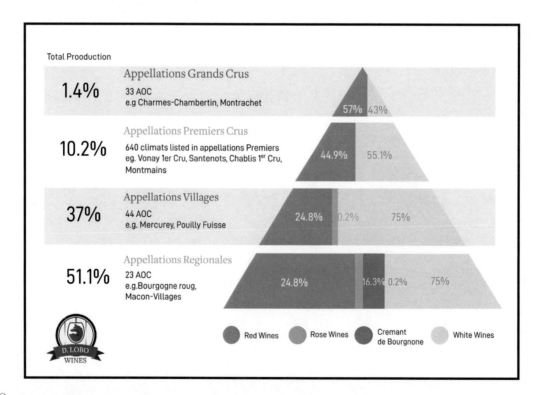

Village wines

For village wines, the totality of the grapes are cultivated in and around the stated village, in this case **Savigny-Lès-Beaune**. In a clever marketing move, many of Burgundy's wine producing villages have appended the name of their most famous vineyard onto the name of the town in order to draw further attention on village wines. But this is not the-case here.

Premier Cru (1er Cru)

For 1er Cru wines, the totality of the grapes originate from a particular vineyard.
In this case, the vineyard's name is **Chassagne-Montrachet**. It is located in the hamlet of Blanchot. Look for the words "Premier Cru" or "1er Cru" on the label.

Single Vineyard Grand Cru

Here, the totality of the grapes that compose this wine come from the very best vineyards of Burgundy. Notice how there is no village name on the label. A Grand Cru will only have **the name of the vineyard** on the label.

Burgundy wine label terminology

Domaine: These are grower/producers that own the same vineyards they are producing wine from. The entire process from growing the grapes to aging and bottling the wine is done by the Domaine itself.

Négociants: Négociants are wine merchants who buy grapes and/or finished wines for blending and bottling under their own label.

Clos: Clos designates a plot of vineyard land traditionally surrounded with dry stone walls. Clos Vougeot, a grand cru vineyard next to the tiny village of Vougeot, is the most famous example.

Monopole (Monopoly): Parcels of vineyard land with a single ownership, monopoles are less common than you might think. Most vineyards in Burgundy have multiple owners.

Lieu-Dit: Term used to describe the location for a specific vineyard that has an established name.

Climat: This term defines a specific parcel or plot located within a vineyard that holds a unique terroir characteristic.

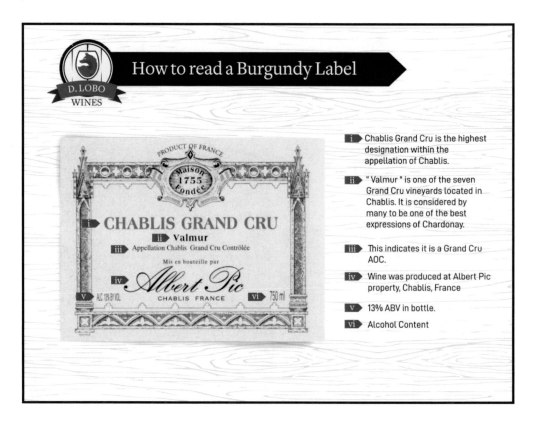

BURGUNDY'S SUB-REGIONS

Chablis

Almost halfway from Paris to Beaune lies the historic wine town of Chablis, right in the Serein River valley. Although it is located in a perfect channel for cold winds and biting frost, its region mostly experiences a cool, continental climate that allows Chardonnay vineyards to thrive. It is in fact in that area that the delicious Chablis, Petit Chablis, Chablis Premier Cru and Chablis Grand Cru AOP white wines are crafted. Essentially, the best yielding grapevines in the region are rooted deep in Kimmeridgian marl, a very fertile limestone and clay blend, brewed together with millions of oyster fossils... Soils that are derived from Kimmeridgian marl are believed to produce wines of excellent quality. Buried under a layer of Portlandien limestone, a younger and purer form of the sedimentary rock, the famed marl was therefore chosen to pave hillsides and elevated plateaus all around Chablis. The Petit Chablis wine most particularly benefits from these cooler plateaus, which undergo an ideal wind exposure.

Counting no less than 17 different wine producing communes, located on both sides of the Serein River, Chablis is the largest white winegrowing region of Bourgogne. In fact, 1 out of 5 bottles of Burgundy (excluding Beaujolais) bear Chablis's name on their label every year. The area's top premiers crus include Montée de Tonnerre and Fourchaume on the right bank of the Serein River, and Vaillons and Montmains on the left. Although there is technically only one Grand Cru appellation in Chablis, the region's Grand Cru AOP has 7 designations in total, encompassing the southwest facing hillsides located above Chablis: Les Clos, Blanchot, Bougros, Grenouilles, Preuses, Valmur and Vaudésir. Number 8, named La Moutonne (which overlapps Vaudésir and Preuses) is allowed by the INAO to appear on labels but is not listed as an official geographic designation.

Convinced that wood, and more specifically oak, compromises the traditional and classic taste of even Chablis's best wines, some vignerons prefer to ferment their wines in stainless steel. New oak therefore only makes its appearance in the production of richer, riper grand cru wines. Either way, the finest Chablis wines are known to taste and smell rather austere in their youth, but become a true delight as they age.

Location and geography

Located 80 miles north of the Côte d'Or, Chablis lies very close to the renowned wine region of Champagne.

Climate

Chablis's climate is described as cool continental climate. Harvesting time in the region is therefore critical, as late frosts may represent a devastating threat.

Soil composition

Chablis' soil is composed of limestone and kimmeridgian clay.

Grape varieties

White
        - Chardonnay

Vinification

Malolactic fermentation is a common practice in the region. This process turns tart malic acid, which is naturally produced by grapes, into softer-tasting lactic acid. Also known as "Malo" or "ML", the process occurs naturally in both red and white wines. ML may add buttery, popcorn and creamy textures to white wines.

Oak is often used with higher-quality wines.

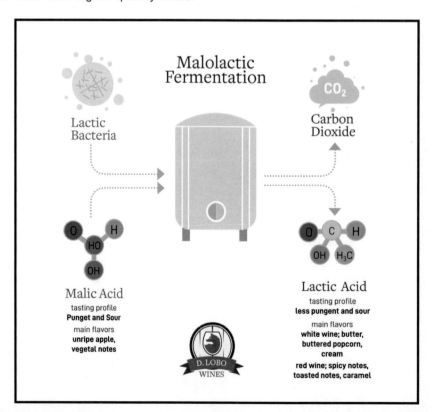

Chablis appellations

- **Chablis AOP**
- **Petit Chablis AOP**
- **Chablis Premier Cru AOP.** 40 vineyards are designated as Premier Cru
- **Chablis Grand Cru AOP**

Seven vineyards designations (most face South to maximize sun exposure):

- Les Clos
Rich and complex, it holds a near-perfect mineral balance.

- Blanchot
Displays delicate floral hints, which makes it the softestof the grands crus.

- Grenouilles
Satisfying and elegant, Grenouilles is also highly aromatic.

- Bougros
Strong flavors.

- Les Preuses
A great balance of complex and buttery.

- Vaudésir
Intense flavors that display notable finesse and spicy hints.

- Valmur
Intense flavors, but soft texture.

Some Chablis producers

- **Domaine François Raveneau**, Chablis, Les Clos Grand Cru
- **Vincent Dauvissat**, Chablis, Les Preuses Grand Cru
- **Samuel Billaud**, Chablis, Vaudésir Grand Cru
- **Domaine William Fèvre**, Chablis, 1er Cru Vaulorent

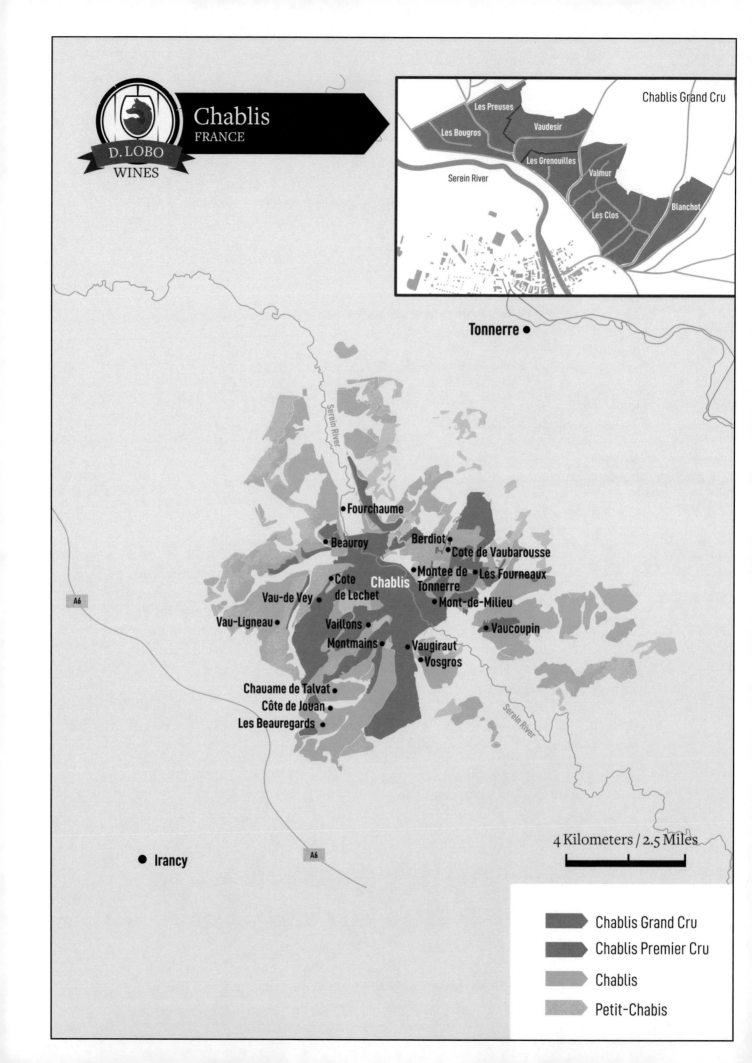

Côte d'Or

Starting near Dijon, the Côte d'Or runs for about 30 miles southward before reaching the village of Santenay. Its narrow ridge of limestone is split into two famous vineyard regions: the Côte de Nuits (North) and the Côte de Beaune (South).

In the language of love, the word "côte" refers to a hillside or a slope. The map indeed shows that the Côte d'Or's villages and vineyards hug said slopes. The latter are an important aspect of the region's terroir, as hillside vinification is known to yield higher quality wines. As a matter of fact, soil composition and microclimates vary depending on vineyard location.

Côte de Nuits (Northen Côte d'Or)

Also known as the Pinot Noir country, the Côte de Nuits region stretches from the outskirts of Dijon to the small town of Corgoloin. The Côte d'Or's village designated red wines include, from north to south, Marsannay, Fixin, Gevrey-Chambertin, Morey-Saint-Denis, Chambolle-Musigny, Vougeot, Vosne-Romanée and Nuits-Saint-Georges. Out of these nine communes, only Marsannay, Fixin, Morey-Saint-Denis, Vougeot and Nuit-Saint-Georges are known to produce – and merely little amounts of - AOP white wines. In total, the Côte de Nuits area shelters 24 Grand Cru vineyards which all produce variations of red wine except for one, Musigny, which also produce whites.

Now, if you are wondering where the best Pinot Noir vineyards are based, you might want to take a trip to Gevrey-Chambertin, just south of little Fixin. In fact, the village of Gevrey-Chambertin itself is home to a total of nine grand cru vineyards, which tops any number of grands crus contained within one town. It is in Gevrey, for short, that savory, "masculine and brooding" Grands Crus Chambertin and Chambertin-Clos de Bèze and Premier Cru Clos Saint-Jacques are produced. Owning over 400 hectares (990 acres) of grapevines, Gevrey-Chambertin is the largest village appellation zone in the Côte d'Or, seven other grands cru appending Chambertin's name to their own...

With that much land, it is safe to say that the Gevrey empire harbors a wide range of quality wines, from second-tier Grands Crus Charmes-Chambertin and Latricières-Chambertin to superior Clos Saint-Jacques (a vineyard that was actually excluded from the Grand Cru classification in 1936 as its borders did not match Chambertin's). With an intense deep color stemming from black fruits, Gevrey-Chambertin's wines display higher concentration and density than those of Vosne-Romanée or Chambolle-Musigny – a silkier, more elegant rouge. We owe this true savoir faire to the presence of highly acclaimed estates in Gevrey, such as Jean-Marie Fourrier, Armand Rousseau and Claud Dugat.

The red wines of Chambolle-Musigny, as mentioned above, tend to emphasize charm and sophistication over the power displayed by an old bottle of Gevrey. Retaining proven intensity and depth nonetheless, Chambolle's wines have a delicate, soft taste that makes them easily gulpable. The village's vinyards produce two grands crus, Musigny and Bonnes-Mares, as well as one outstanding premier cru: Les Amoureuses. It is also home to some greatly esteemed addresses like Georges de Vogüé, Ghislaine Barthod, Georges et Christophe Roumier and Perrot-Minot.

Moving on to Morey-Saint-Denis, any wine aficionado will notice that it is a perfect merging-point between Gevrey and Chambolle wines, which have two rather polarized crafts and styles. Containing elements of both, the Morey-Saint-Denis region is home to the four grands crus Clos the Tart, Clos de Lambrays, Clos de la Roche and Clos Saint-Denis and to a flake of a fifth, Bonnes-Mares. Domaines Dujac and Ponsot are two of the area's top estates.

As villages pile up in rural France, it would be quite easy to overlook the small town of Vougeot if it wasn't for the splendid Château de Clos de Vougeot... Majestically standing among the vineyards, this Renaissance built castle is one of Burgundy's most emblematic landmarks, although it doesn't absolve the Clos de Vougeot from the critiques it is addressed. Indeed, the area's 50 hectares (124 acres) of vineyards (the largest Grand Cru in the Côte de Nuits) and its significant number of growers lead to very incohesive quality patterns. Consequently, only four premiers crus are produced on the large vineyard: Clos de la Perrière, Les Petits Vougeots, Les Cras and le Clos Blanc. Occupying over 80% of the village's vine land, there is only limited room for premier cru or even village-level designated production.

As Chambolle and Gevrey wines prove themselves to be superior blends, the esteemed grands crus of Vosne-Romanée offer them a fierce competition.

Containing the most praised samples of Pinot Noir, Vosne's wines are archetypes of authentic craft and aristocratic precision while preserving an inherent copiousness. And with great wines usually comes fewer outputs, the smallest in the region (and in France) being La Romanée, a monopole held by the Comte Liger-Belair, at only 0.85 planted hectares (2 acres). Along with Grand Cru La Grande Rue, owned by Domaine François Lamarche, Domaine de la Romanée-Conti's grands crus La Tâche and namesake Romanée-Conti equate as monopoles too. Richebourg and Romanée-Saint-Vivant, larger in size and

owned by several entities, complete Vosne's grands crus selection, making room for its also acclaimed collection of premiers crus. Top sites include Vosne-Romanée, Les Suchots, Les Beaux Monts and Les Petits Monts, Aux Malconsorts and Cros Parantoux (the latter dignified by Henri Jayer). Each premier cru in Vosne-Romanée is known to share a border with a grand cru, except for the monopole Clos des Réas, owned by Michel Gros. Furthermore, a lot of Burgundy's most esteemed red wine producers work directly in the commune of Vosne-Romanée, such as Romanée-Conti and Comte Liger-Belair, as well as Domaine Leroy, Anne Gros, Jean Grivot, Meó Camuzet and others.

With such a reputable name, Vosne-Romanée even lends its appellation to the Flagey-Echézaux village. The latter does not have its own designation even though it is home to two grands crus, Echézeaux and Grands-Echézeaux. Flagey-Echézeaux also contains some premier cru vineyards, making up a total of 35 hectares (86 acres) and 80 individual parcels. A structure that suffers from the very same judgments as Clos de Vougeot. Too many vignerons share the land, which equates in too many quality variations and no consistent theme of terroir. Luckily, the smaller, triangular Grands-Echézeaux vineyard holds a universally praised status and is therefore priced accordingly.

Between northern Vosne-Romanée and southern Premeaux-Prissey belongs Nuits-Saint-Georges and its sturdy wines, that come both from Nuits-Saint-Georges itself and from its neighbor Premeaux. Closer to Vosne, Nuits-Saint-Georges's bottles unfold a soft and fruity character. Nearer Premeaux, the wines are described as fuller and richer... Quality wines that owe their singularity to expert artisans Henri Gouges, Joseph Faiveley Jean-Jacques Confuron and Robert Chevillon. Nuits-Saint-Georges has no current grands crus – the last being La Grand Rue in Vosne-Romanée (promoted in 1992) - but still shelters promising premiers crus such as Les Saint-Georges, a vineyard that holds a lot of potential.

South of Nuits-Saint-Georges lie Comblanchien and Corgoloin, two villages that are entitled only to the Côte de Nuits-Villages appellation, and the beginning of the Côte de Beaune.

QUICK FACTS

Climate

Côte de Nuits's climate is continental.

Topography and aspect

The region's landscape displays hillsides and cliffs. Top vineyard sites are often lie in a hillside's center.

Soil composition

Limestone and Marl compose the soil of Côte de Nuits.

Grape varieties

Red
- Pinot Noir

Viticulture

The region faces threats of frost, summer hail, and excessive rain in the fall.

Vinification

Wine makers in the are use mostly new French oak. Some producers ferment with whole grape clusters, others completely de-stem their crops.

Village appellations

100% of the grapes are grown in and around the named village. There are 9 villages in the Côte de Nuits: **Marsannay, Fixin, Gevrey-Chambertin, Morey-Saint-Denis, Chambolle-Musigny, Vougeot, Vosne-Romanée, Flagey-Echézeaux, Nuits-Saint-Georges.**

Appellations and styles

Premier Cru AOP

100% of the grapes are grown in an individually named premier cru vineyard. If no name appears on the label, the wine may be a blend of grapes from any of the premier cru vineyards in that villages. There are more than 130 premier cru vineyards in the Côte de Nuits.

Grand Cru AOP

100% of the grapes are grown in the named grand cru vineyard site. 24 of 33 grand cru sites in Burgundy are in the Côte de Nuits.

Grand Cru vineyards

- La Tâche
- La Romanée
- Musigny
- Bonnes-Mares
- Chambertin

Top recent vintages of Côte de Nuits

2005, 2009, 2010, 2014, 2015.

Some Côtes de Nuits producers

- Armand Rousseau
- Aurélien Verdet
- Christian Sérafin
- Comtes Lafon
- Denis Mortet
- Domaine de la Romanée-Conti
- Etienne Sauzet
- Henri Jayer

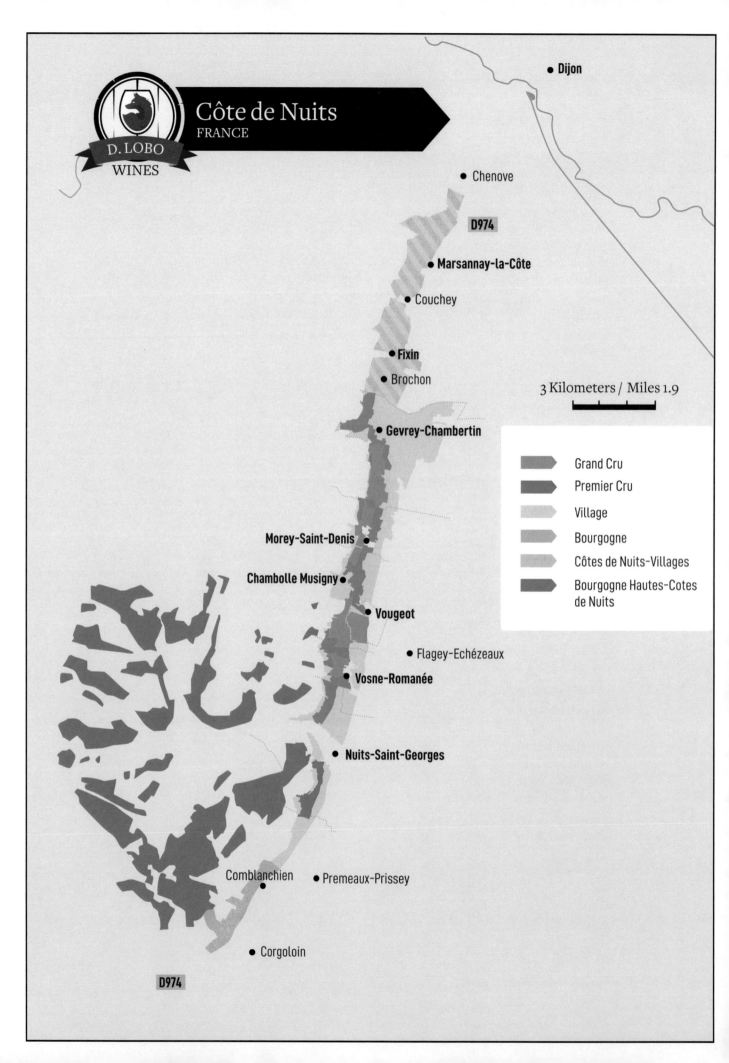

Côte de Beaune (Southern Côte d'Or)

Just south of the Côte de Nuits's border rolls out another one of France's reputable côtes: the Côte de Beaune. As one drives south from the city of Corgoloin, one discovers the spectacular lush hill of Corton which, stretching across the landscape, marks the starting point of Côte de Beaune. While the hill's crown is made of trees, its flanks are composed of 160 hectares (395 acres) of Pinot Noir and Chardonnay vineyards, all labeled as Corton AOP. Three communes share the southern half of the hill: Aloxe-Corton, Ladoix-Serrigny and Pernand-Vergelesses.

Today, Corton's vineyards both produce red and white wines, and folktales tell us we owe it to Charlemagne. Legend has it that in the late 700s, King Charlemagne ordered red grapevines to be planted on the hill of Corton after watching the snow melt off its slopes. As the ruler aged his beard whitened, and so did Corton's wine. Charlemagne's wife, shameful of the ruby stains on his silver beard, convinced him to swap his beloved rouge to a more discreet white... And that wraps up the story behind Corton-Charlemagne and Charlemagne grands crus that, bearing the Frankish king's name, only produce white wines. That being said, the Corton appellation also allows the output of red wines, which actually are predominant on the hill. In fact, Corton is the sole red wine producing grand cru in the Côte the Beaune and is the largest single Grand Cru appellation in the entire region of Burgundy! But as we have seen previously, "largest" certainly doesn't equate to "greatest". Corton Rouge is in fact the least expensive grand cru, as it suffers from uncertain managing and quality. The hill's vineyards would probably have been better off as premiers crus... And although Corton-Charlemagne AOP white wines are considered valuable, they seldom reach France's top grands crus's level. Admittingly silky and rich, Corton's Chardonnay wines unfortunately don't own the depth of an excellent Montrachet.

As the commercial capital of Burgundy, Beaune reveals itself as the perfect place for négociant activity and for estates like Joseph Drouhin, Bouchard Père et Fils, and Louis Jadot to exist. While Beaune has no grands crus, it boasts more planted hectares than any other city in the Côte de Beaune and harbors 42 premier cru vineyards. In fact, about 85% of Beaune's planted acres are premiers crus and the rest of them, village vineyards like Les Bressandes, Grèves and Clos des mouches, are some of the most sophisticated ones. Besides, only a few hectares of grapevines above Beaune are classified as Côte de Beaune AOP.

After Corton's, the most full-bodied rouge of the Côte de Beaune would be that of Pommard (AOP), which displays a vigorous, tannic composition. Excellent premier cru sources in and around Pommard include Les Rugiens and les Epenots, two vineyards that belong to one of the Côte de Beaune's best monopoles: Comte Armand's Clos des Epeneaux. Contrastingly, the neighboring town of Volnay (often associated with Pommard when talking about one or the other) offers red wines with softer fragrances and a tad more charm. Les Caillerets, Champans, Clos des Chênes, Taillepieds and Clos des Ducs all represent the town's finer premiers crus. As for "best producers", the medal goes to Marquis d'Angerville (which owns monopole Clos des Ducs), Hubert de Montille and Michel Lafarge. Depending on the color of the wine, a few surrounding premiers crus may be labeled as Volnay's, like Meursault's vineyards for instance. Adjoining Volnay's border, Meursault's vines can be certified "Volnay Premier Cru Santenots" if bearing Pinot Noir instead of Chardonnay grapes.

Of course, the Côte de Beaune also provides a selection of excellent white wines, produced in the villages of Meursault, Puligny-Montrachet and Chassagne-Montrachet to name a few. Out of those three towns, Meursault is undoubtedly the most productive, as it crafts a higher quantity of white wines than any other hamlet in all of the Côte d'Or. Needless to say, Meursault's wines also show great quality with a soft nutty and buttery, almost fat on the tongue and palate, array of flavors. Having no grand cru vineyard is not a worry for Meursault, since a number of its premiers crus – Perrières, Les Genevrières, Les Charmes... - can easily reach superior cru quality. Another specificity of Meursault is that its village wines have long been designated by lieu-dit, or "deuxième cru", meaning that named vineyards such as Les Narvaux or Les Chevalières appear on labels, but the wines are still seen as village-level rather than premier cru. Domaines Coche-Dury, Guy Roulot and Comtes Lafon are three of Meursault's most acclaimed vineyards.

The highest priced and refined white wines, however, come from Montrachet and its two most prominent vineyards, Puligny-Montrachet and Chassagne-Montrachet.

The Montrachet empire further lengthens: on the slope above lies the grand cru Chevalier-Montrachet (located right in Puligny), and below belongs Bâtard-Montrachet, Bienvenues-Bâtard-Montrachet (near Puligny) and Criots-Bâtard-Montrachet (near Chassagne), the latter being the smallest of all white grands crus. The small village of Blagny, which produces red wines under its very own AOP label, also bottles quality white wines, but as either Meursault or Puligny-Montrachet (depending on the vineyard's location).

Symbolizing some of the world's most age-worthy examples of Chardonnay, Montrachet expertly preserves a balance of depth, concentration and sourness unseen in any other grand cru white wines. In contrast to Meursault's rounder nature for instance, Puligny-Montrachet's wines are tauter, more streamlined and usually treated to less new oak. Puligny's best premiers crus would be Les Pucelles, Le Cailleret and Les Demoiselles, all sharing border with some grands crus. The most esteemed artisans? Domaine Leflaive and Jacques Carillon, without a doubt.

On the other hand, Chassagne-Montrachet's turnouts can be a bit more complex to describe, since the commune arranged more red than white wines until the 1980's. By now, it is safe to affirm that Chassagne's wines are closer in style and tastes to a soft Meursault than to a hard-edged Puligny. In total, Chassagne boasts two major Domaines – Ramonet and Pierre-Yves Colin-Morey – and 55 premiers crus, which is more than any other single town in the Côte d'Or. A lot of small sites, however, are grouped within larger ones, such as the Premier Cru Morgeot, and its 15 smaller planted acres. All of these little sites usually sell their bottles under Morgeot's better-known title.

As a result of its larger size, the Côte de Beaune covers a lot more village-level vineyards than the Côte de Nuits, some that might be lesser known but that still hold significant value or potential. For instance, you might have heard of white and red wine producing villages Auxey-Duresses, Maranges, Monthélie, Saint-Aubin, Chorey-Lès-Beaune and Saint-Romain, all geographically labeled as premiers crus except for the last two.

Climate

Côte de Beaune enjoys a continental climate with a spectrum of microclimates that differ from village to village, and sometimes even vineyard to vineyard.

Soil composition

The region's soil is made of Limestone and Marl.

Grape varieties

White
- Chardonnay

Red
- Pinot Noir

Vinificitation

Producers in the region use oak, often new, for both reds and whites.

Village appellations

100% of the grapes are grown in and around the named village. Here are some of the best known named villages:

- **Aloxe-Corton**
- **Pommard**
- **Volnay**
- **Meursault**
- **Puligny**
- **Montrachet**
- **Chassagne-Montrachet**
- **Ladoix**
- **Serrigny**
- **Chorey-Les-Beaune**
- **Savigny-Lès-Beaune**
- **Monthélie**
- **Auxey-Duresses**
- **Santenay**
- **Beaune**

Regional appellations

Premier Cru AOP

100% of of the grapes come from an individually named premier cru vineyard. As for Côte de Nuits wines, if no vineyard name is on the label, the wine can be a blend of grapes.

Grand Cru AOP

100% of the grapes are grown in the named grand cru vineyard site. 8 of Burgundy's grand cru vineyards are situated in the Côte de Beaune.

- **Corton**
- **Corton-Charlemagne**
- **Charlemagne**
- **Montrachet**
- **Chevalier-Montrachet**
- **Bâtard-Montrachet**
- **Bienvenues-Bâtard-Montrachet**
- **Criots-Bâtard-Montrachet**

Some Côte de Beaune producers

- **Leflaive**
- **Leroy**
- **Jacques-Frédéric Mugnier**
- **Joseph Drouhin**
- **Philippe Colin**
- **Ramonet**

Top recent vintages of Côte de Beaune

2005, 2009, 2010, 2014, 2015.

For your culture

A year in Burgundy, 2013. A movie by David Kennard

Côte de Beaune
FRANCE

D. LOBO WINES

4 Kilometers / 2.5 Miles

- Grand Cu
- Premier Cru
- Village
- Bourgeogne
- Bourgeogne Hautes-Côtes de Beaune

D974

Pernand-Vergelesses •
Savigny-lès-Beaune • • Ladoix
Aloxe-Corton

• Chorey-lès-Beaune

Beaune •

Pommard •
Volnay •
Saint-Romain •   Monthélie •
Auxey Duresses •

Meursault •

Blagny •
Saint-Aubin •
• Puligny-Montrachet

Chassagne-Montrachet •

Dezize-lès-Maranges •   • Santenay
Sampigny-lès-Maranges •
Cheilly-lès-Maranges •

D974

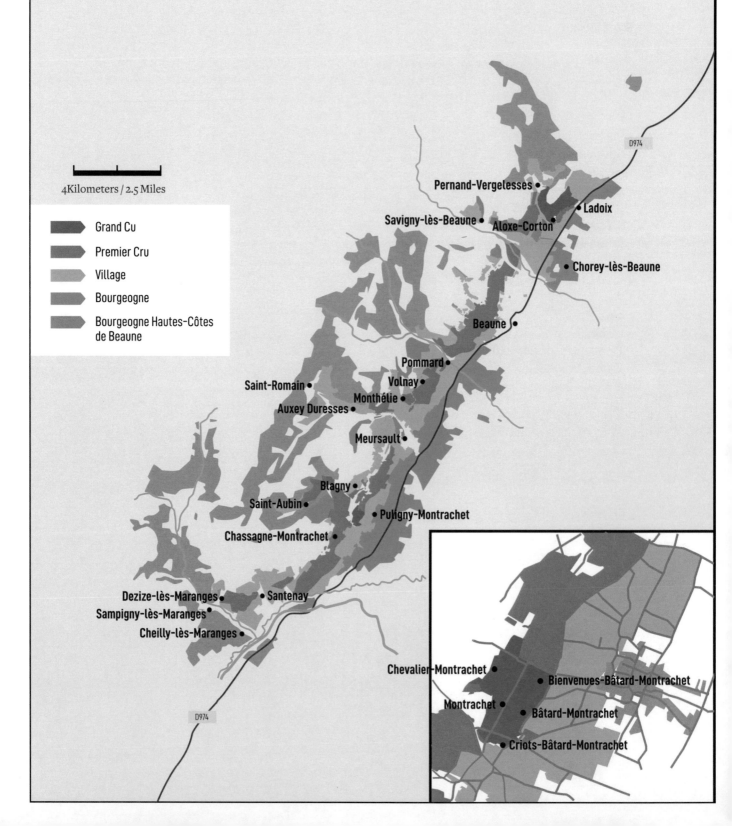

Chevalier-Montrachet •
• Bienvenues-Bâtard-Montrachet
Montrachet •
• Bâtard-Montrachet
• Criots-Bâtard-Montrachet

Côte Chalonnaise

With soils resembling the Côte de Beaune's, the Côte Chalonnaise forms a 25-kilometer belt along the western border of the Saône River valley. Sloping but somewhat smooth – or at least less jagged than Beaune's hills, the Côte Chalonnaise experience cool winds that tend to delay ripening and harvesting times. Furthermore, there is no continuous sea of vineyards like the Côte d'Or's, meaning that the Chalonnaise vines are all dispersed on different hillsides and villages, making it hard for the region's economy or even culture to depend greatly on its red, white and rosé winemaking. In fact, the Côte Chalonnaise and its 44 winegrowing communes only became an official geographic designation of the Bourgogne AOP in 1990!

Nonetheless, five of Bourgogne-Côte Chalonnaise's villages achieved to make a name for themselves and gained their very own appellations:

- **Bouzeron**
- **Givry**
- **Mercurey**
- **Montagny**
- **Rully**

While Montagny and Bouzeron (Burgundy's only village-level appellation that make wines from the Aligoté grape) only produce white wines; Givry, Mercurey and Rully can bottle either white or red. The latter town, a well-known source of quality Chardonnay, was Burgundy's sparkling wines birthplace in the 19th century. Today, the village still prevails as the main artisan of Crémant de Bourgogne AOP. As for the Givry and Mercurey vineyards, they are both established as the best rouge producers in the region and work far more with Pinot Noir than with Chardonnay grapes. About two-thirds of the Côte Chalonnaise's crops come from Mercurey alone.

Location and geography

The Côte Chalonnaise is directly south of the Côte d'Or, but does not display any hillsides that protect the vineyards from harsh eastern winds.

Climate

The region enjoys a continental climate.

Soil composition

Limestone is the main component of the region's soils.

Grape varieties

White
- Chardonnay
- Aligoté (in small volume)

Red
- Pinot Noir

Vinification

Little to no oak is used for both whites and reds.

Village appellations

- **Bouzeron AOP.** White wine only – Aligoté
- **Rully AOP.** White, red and sparkling wine
    - Chardonnay
    - Pinot Noir
    - Crémant de Bourgogne
- **Mercurey AOP.** White and red wine
    - Chardonnay
    - Pinot Noir
- **Givry AOP.** White and red wine
    - Chardonnay
    - Pinot Noir
- **Montagny AOP.** White wine only
    – Chardonnay

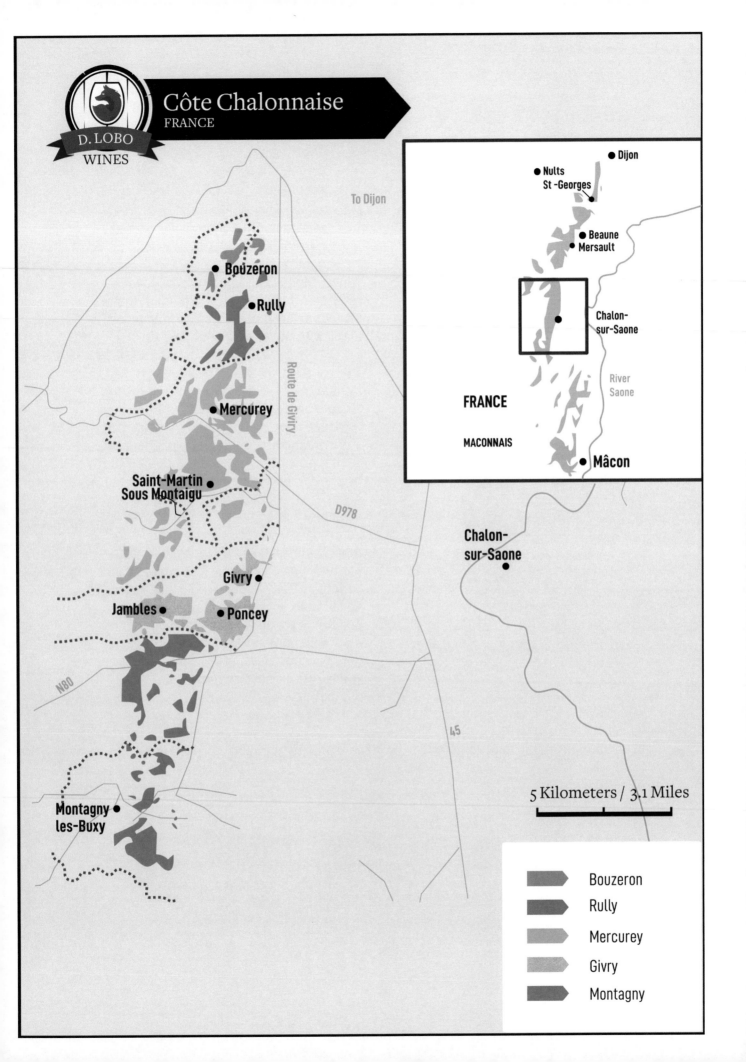

Mâconnais

Also known as the Chardonnay country, the Mâconnais region is Burgundy's second biggest white wine producer, after Chablis. While the village of Chardonnay produces the namesake grape as well as a few red Gamay wines, the Mâcon AOP vineyards - 25 kilometers away — yield white, red (including varietally labeled Gamay) and rosé wines. Most Chardonnays produced in Mâcon, fruitier and lighter than Chablis's, are fermented in stainless steel, with not one trace of oak.

The Mâcon AOP classification is available to all artisans of the Mâconnais region, although 85% of its turnout is usually labeled with the Mâcon-Villages geographic appellation. To be precise, single communes will generally geographically label their wines by appending their name to Mâcon's, such as Lugny, Milly-Lamartine, Pierreclos and about 20 others. And if many of those may yield all three types of wines, only whites can benefit from the Mâcon-Villages appellation. Interestingly enough, cafés and bistros seem to have the upper and unofficial hand on Mâcon's most prized golden wines, particularly those labeled with a geographic appellation. A tough competition for the Côte d'Or vignerons, who now tend to travel southward in the quest of more affordable land.

In addition to the regional appellation, the Mâconnais has five village appellations:

- **Pouilly-Fuissé**
- **Pouilly-Loché**
- **Pouilly-Vinzelles**
- **Saint-Véran**
- **Viré-Clessé**

All five produce only Chardonnay. Pouilly-Fuissé includes the wines of four communes:

- **Fuissé**
- **Solutré-Pouilly**
- **Vergisson**
- **Chaintré**

Those vineyards ornate the slopes below the Rocks of Solutré and Vergisson, two large limestone cliffs that define the Mâconnais's southern landscape – the most praised winegrowing area in the region. The Mâconnais AOP designation was actually one of the first French white wines to become a staple on refined mid-1900s American tables.

Moreover, the AOP vineyards of Saint-Véran also hold a highly regarded status, rivaling with Pouilly-Fuissé's both in production size and in reputation. The last AOP on the list, Viré-Clessé, earns the medal for Mâcon's youngest designation. Born in 1999, the Viré-Clessé AOP label covers the wines of two villages.

Climate

Although Mâconnais's climate is overall continental, it gets slightly warmer and drier than in the other northern Burgundy areas.

Topography

It is a fairly large area displaying low hills and flatter terrain.

Grape varieties

White
- Chardonnay

Red
- Pinot Noir
- Gamay

Vinification

The region mainly produces white wines. Producers use very little new oak aside for the wines of Pouilly-Fuissé. There are no grand or premier cru vineyards in the Mâconnais, but the main villages (listed below) brandish their own AOP.

Village appellations

- **Mâcon AOP**
- **Saint-Veran AOP**
- **Pouilly-Fuissé AOP**, which includes the wines of four communes:
        - **Fuissé**
        - **Solutré-Pouilly**
        - **Vergisson**
        - **Chaintré**
- **Pouilly-Loché AOP**
- **Pouilly-Vinzelles AOP**
- **Viré-Clessé AOP**

Some Mâconnais producers

- **Daniel Barraud**
- **Robert-Denogent**
- **Roger Lassarat**
- **Valette**
- **J.A. Ferret**

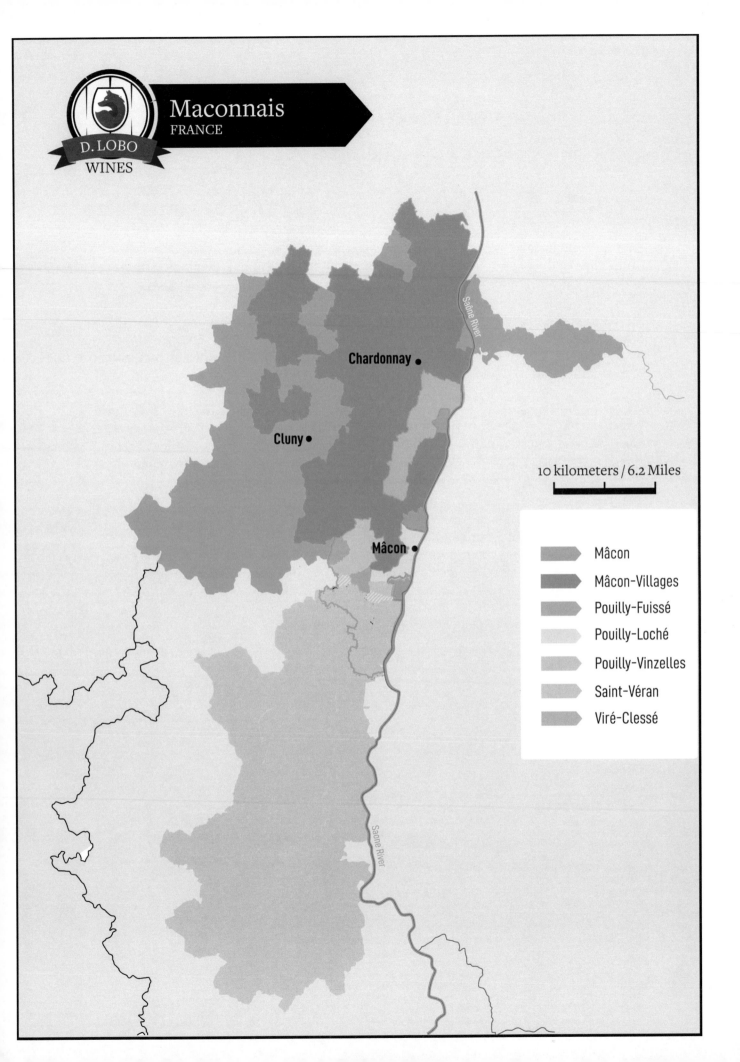

Maconnais
FRANCE

D. LOBO
WINES

Saône River

Chardonnay •

Cluny •

Mâcon •

10 kilometers / 6.2 Miles

Saône River

Mâcon
Mâcon-Villages
Pouilly-Fuissé
Pouilly-Loché
Pouilly-Vinzelles
Saint-Véran
Viré-Clessé

Beaujolais

Slightly overlapping the southern Mâconnais, the region of Beaujolais is the last of Burgundy's. A large part of its territory stretches all the way to the Rhône department and close to Lyon, France's true capital of gastronomy and third most populated city.

Although some Chardonnay and Pinot Noir may hide among Beaujolais's vines, the predominantly red wine growing region could very well be rebaptized "Gamay empire", as a whopping 98% of its planted acres favor this specific type of grapes. In fact, half of the world's Gamay parcels belong to the region...

Beaujolais is home to 12 excellent AOPs, such as namesake Beaujolais AOP, the Beaujolais-Villages AOP and the 10 other northern cru AOPs. The bulk of Beaujolais AOPs are crafted in the flatter, limestone and clay soils of the region's southern parts. These fertile grounds provide tasty Chardonnay, known as Bourgogne or Beaujolais Blanc as well as entry-level Gamay reds, most of southern Beaujolais's rouge turnout being fairly recent.

Beaujolais-Villages AOP on the other hand, produce all three colors of wines on more rugged, granite hillsides (monts de Beaujolais), resulting in intense, complex and riper wines. In total, the designation covers 38 northern and central villages and offer delectable, reputable crus.

Beaujolais's 10 other esteemed AOP appellations include:

- **Saint-Amour**
- **Juliénas**
- **Moulin-à-Vent**
- **Chénas, Fleurie**
- **Chiroubles**
- **Morgon**
- **Régnié**
- **Brouilly**
- **Côte de Brouilly**

Although grown and produced rather close to one another, these 10 wines can vary exceedingly in style. While Chiroubles is known for its light and supple wines, Moulin-à-vent yields darker, tannic wines. As different as they can be, however, all of these wines prove themselves to be true age-worthy values of modern Burgundy. Beaujolais's wine artisans are in fact known to hand-harvest their crops with a rare passion and respect for old traditions. And when the Côte d'Or witnessed loosened regulations on maximum yields, Beaujolais's vignerons actually rigidified theirs. Their internationally recognized dedication did not, however, stop the region's overall image from being tarnished by the rise in popularity of Beaujolais Nouveau wines – less complex, and put on the market very early, only a few weeks after the harvest. First launched in 1950, the release of those nouveau wines only became famous around the 70s and allowed Beaujolai's largest producer Georges Dubœuf's name to get propelled among other famous maisons.

Nonetheless, parts of the region still maintain valuable savoir faire, such as prominent carbonic and semi-carbonic maceration techniques for the production of red wines specifically. Carbonic maceration works like so: vinificators throw whole clusters of red grapes in a tank, then seal it and inject carbon dioxide to displace oxygen. In an oxygen free environment, whole berries of grapes undergo a short, intracellular fermentation. This process helps metabolizing a grape's glucose and malic acid to produce alcohol without using yeast. During the maceration process, each grape's skin release tannins and anthocyanins into their flesh, giving color to the juice. Before the grape and its cells die, it can develop an alcohol level of about 2%. Then, if the grapes don't burst on their own due to internal build-up of carbon dioxide, the winemaker will press them to acquire their juice. Either way, the wine will ferment to dryness, emulating the normal effects of yeast.

In Beaujolais, winemakers tend to prefer the semi-carbonic maceration method. In this case, whole clusters laying at the bottom of the tub are crushed under the weight of the ones above and begin fermenting naturally, meaning that carbon dioxide gets released from the squashed fruit. Additional gas thus does not need to be pumped in, as the carbon dioxide produced by the macerating fruit causes the top clusters to ferment internally. This technique generally suppresses the strong yeast notes we can taste in young wines, which may actually be the root of those unconventional "bubblegum" or "pear-drop" flavors that are often cited as evidence of carbonic maceration. It is true though, that wines resulting from any type of carbonic maceration often taste fruitier, sweeter and more floral than other wines. Nevertheless, carbonic maceration has long been implemented by many wine artisans in northern Beaujolais, but also in other areas of France - like the Rhône and the Loire valleys -, as well as in Spain and in California.

Lastly, you will find savory Coteaux-du-Lyonnais AOP in the south of Beaujolais, close to the city of Vienne in the north of the Rhône valley, where the climate and wines surprisingly resemble northern Beaujolais's. All red, white and rosé wines are produced on the vineyard, red and rosé being drawn from Gamay grapes, and whites containing Aligoté, Chardonnay and Pinot Blanc. Following the high culinary standards of Lyon, a slightly chilled glass of Gamay perfectly pairs with a traditional andouillette sausage or a classic "Salade Lyonnaise".

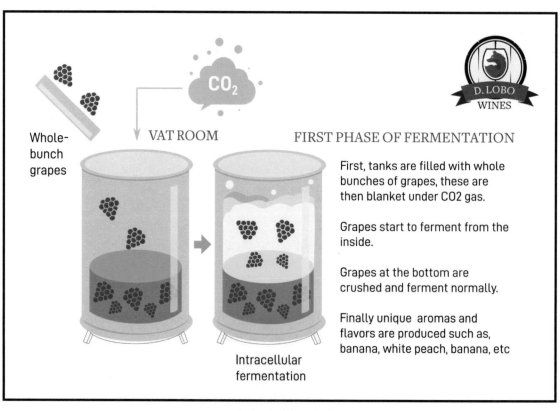

Carbonic fermentation

Location and geography

Beaujolais lies south of, and is slightly overlapping the Mâconnais. It runs for 35 miles from north to south.

Climate

The region's climate is continental.

Soil composition

Schist and granite can be found in the north Beaujolais Cru villages, sandstone and clay can be found in the south.

Grape varieties

White
- Chardonnay (in small volume)

Red
- Gamay

Viticulture

Hillside vineyards with low yields lie in the northern Beaujolais Crus, and flatter plains compose the south of the region.

Vinification

Stainless steel is used by many producers in Beaujolais, and older French oak barrels may be used on occasion. The Carbonic maceration method is also performed.

Regional appellations and styles

- Beaujolais AOP
Made from grapes grown anywhere in the region.

- Beaujolais Nouveau
These easy drinking red wines are released on the third Thursday in November following the harvest. Meant for youthful consumption.

-Beaujolais-Villages AOP
There are 38 designated villages. The wines do not have individual village names on the labels and are simply designated as villages.

- Beaujolais Crus
The region's best wines. 10 named villages, each with their own AOP designation. Red wines are only made from Gamay grapes. Hillside vineyards. Granite soil.

- **Saint-Amour**
- **Chénas**
- **Moulin-à-Vent**
- **Morgon**
- **Côte de Brouilly**
- **Brouilly**
- **Régnié**
- **Chiroubles**
- **Fleurie**
- **Juliénas**

Some Beaujolais producers

- **Dominique Piron**
- **Marcel La Pierre**
- **Julien Sunier**
- **Jean-Paul Brun**
- **Michel Tête**

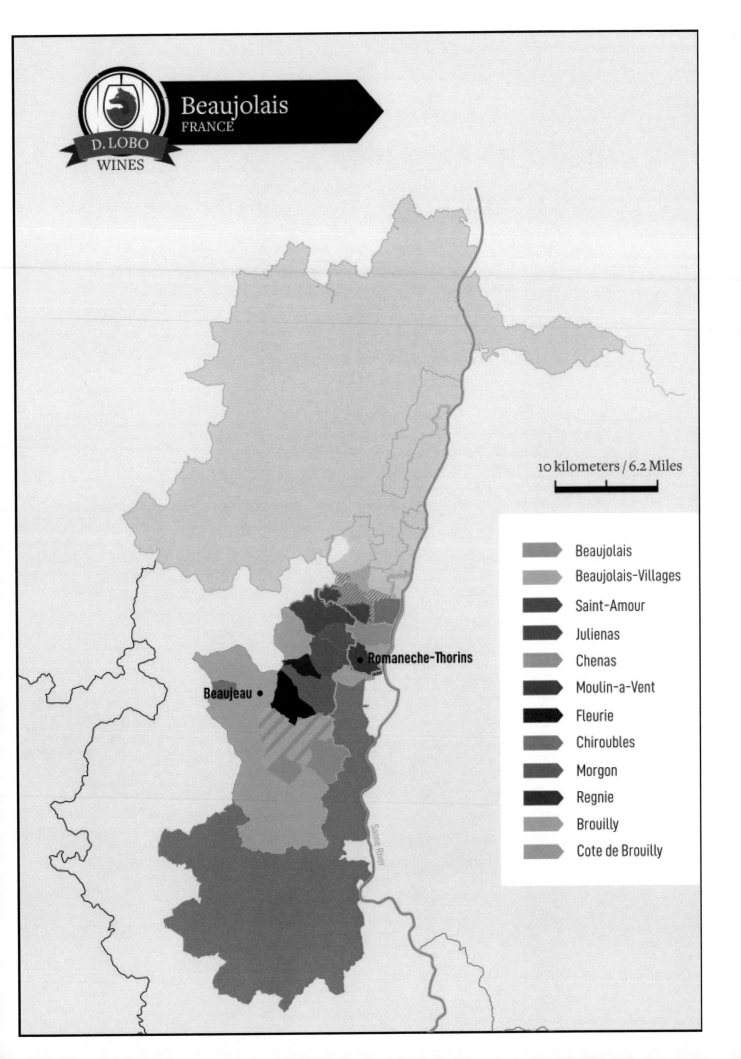

A GLANCE AT BORDEAUX

Historical background

Let's now take a few steps back and observe 4th century Gironde, southwestern department of France and home of Bordeaux. It was around this era that the first clues of viticulture in the region was discovered. Oddly enough, an Ausonius poem is sometimes used as tangible evidence that vignerons were already hard at work in the 300s...

> *"I've never written for a fasting man;*
> *A taste of wine is good before my verse"*

> **...the Roman poet wrote.**

Yet, the wine regions abutting the Garonne river only gained public esteem in the mid-17th century, when the ambitious Dutch skillfully designed a complex swamp draining system throughout the Médoc region. This massive groundwork evidently enhanced the area's wine growing, developed livability, and therefore made the Médoc a prominent wine county.

From 1152 to 1453, Bordeaux was ruled by England, whose crown took a fascination for Bordeaux reds, that they baptized "Claret wines". Clever and enterprising, Dutch traders later fell in love with the famed French rouge as well, and took advantage of Bordeaux's proximity to the Atlantic Ocean to further boost the city's status in international distribution.

After turning the region's salt marshes into profitable vineyards and habitable land, the Nobles of the Robe of France's Ancien Régime settled and instituted some of the esteemed châteaux we know of today. When the commerce in Bordeaux expanded in the 1700s, and a new merchant – négociant - class surfaced. Serving as intermediaries, they would buy grapes in bulk or barreled wine to age in their own cellars before selling it in bottles.

The négociant influence only grew dim after the second World War, supplanted in part by Domaine bottling (bottling of the wine by the producing estates themselves, on their territory). Wine brokers – courtiers – however, also became a powerful authority in the 18th century and very much remained one even after the war. By providing early cash flows and guaranteed wine sales to châteaux, Bordeaux's courtiers gained total control over wine trading. Pioneers of the current "en primeur" sales, wine brokers sell Bordeaux wines while they are still aging in barrel and reaching their expected potential before they become available.

Landmark: La Cité du Vin

"La Cité du Vin" is a wine museum in Bordeaux. Inaugurated in 2016, Bordeaux's wine museum has become one of the city's key touristic attractions. The beautiful building serves as a cultural and patrimonial center revolving around winemaking throught centuries and from around the world. Adopting some theme-park like aspects, La Cité du Vin hosts permanent and temporary exhibitions, workshops and even engaging theatrical perfomances.

Location and geography

Bordeaux is located in Southwestern France, inland from the Atlantic Ocean.

Climate

Bordeaux's climate is maritime, but becomes more continental near Saint-Émilion and Pomerol. Winters are short, springtime is damp and summers can reach high temperatures.

The Atlantic Ocean and the Gironde estuary breeze shield the grapevines of Bordeaux from winter and spring frost, and coastal pine forests insulate the Médoc vineyards from harsh winds that come from the west and northwest. The only thing that cannot be stopped is rain, which is a worry, especially during harvest season, as humidity can cause devastating mold and rot. Autumnal humidity helps develop what is called "noble rot" in the sweet wine region of Graves, but a dreadful drop in temperatures can result in destructive mold that directly impacts the fruit. As for springtime frost, it can lead to coulure (no fertilization) and millerandage (poor fertilization) which can significantly reduce the eventual yield and greatly affect the wine's taste. The Bordeaux mixture of lime, copper sulfate and water is therefore sprayed throughout the region to avoid fungal issues.

Geographical and climatic influences

- A large pine forest along the coast protects the region from the Atlantic's impressive storms and harsh winds.
- The Gironde estuary is formed the Garonne and Dordogne rivers, which meet north of the city of Bordeaux.
- These bodies of water divide the area into three sections:

  - **Left Bank**, west of Garonne and Gironde
  - **Right Bank**, east and north of the Dordogne and Gironde
  - **Entre-deux-Mers**, between the Garonne and Dordogne

Soil composition

Each of Bordeaux's regions has its own specific soil type, matched with the grape varieties that grow best there. Water drainage is key.

- **Médoc** and **Graves** on the **Left Bank** have gravel soil, which suits perfectly with Cabernet Sauvignon, being the primary grape in the wines from this part of the region.
- **Pomerol** and **Saint-Émilion** on the **Right Bank** have sand, clay, and limestone soil, which suits perfectly with Merlot, being the primary grape in the wines from this part of the region.

Grape varieties

White
- Sauvignon Blanc. Offers pungency, high acidity, and citrus flavors.
- Sémillon. Adds body, depth, and concentration.
- Muscadelle. Imparts lovely, and intense floral character.

Red
- Cabernet Sauvignon. Offers the wine structure, power, and longevity.
- Cabernet Franc. Imparts herbal spice, red fruit, and tannins.
- Merlot. The mostly widely planted. Contributes a fleshly, juicy texture
- Malbec. Can soften the austerity of Cabernet Sauvignon.
- Petit Verdot. Offers color, depth, and exotic perfume.
- Carménère. Also allowed but rarely seen.

Viticulture

This region suffers from rain at harvest and frost.

Vinification

Red wines from Bordeaux are usually blends of two or more grape varieties, such as:

- **Cabernet Sauvignon**
- **Cabernet Franc**
- **Merlot**
- **Malbec**
- **Petit Verdot**

- In the left bank, Cabernet Sauvignon is the dominant grape variety in its blends.
- In the right bank, Merlot and Cabernet Franc are the dominant grape varieties used in its blends.

White wines from Bordeaux are usually blends of those grape varieties:

- **Sauvignon Blanc**
- **Sémillon**
- **Muscadelle**

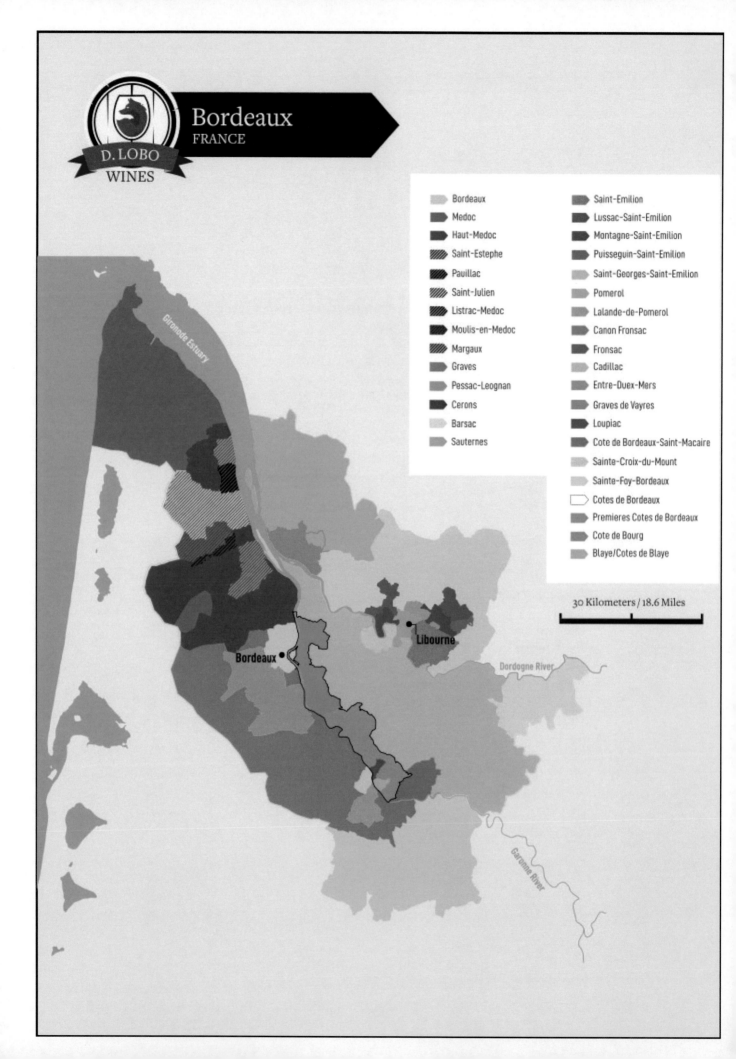

Bordeaux
FRANCE

D. LOBO WINES

Legend:
- Bordeaux
- Medoc
- Haut-Medoc
- Saint-Estephe
- Pauillac
- Saint-Julien
- Listrac-Medoc
- Moulis-en-Medoc
- Margaux
- Graves
- Pessac-Leognan
- Cerons
- Barsac
- Sauternes
- Saint-Emilion
- Lussac-Saint-Emilion
- Montagne-Saint-Emilion
- Puisseguin-Saint-Emilion
- Saint-Georges-Saint-Emilion
- Pomerol
- Lalande-de-Pomerol
- Canon Fronsac
- Fronsac
- Cadillac
- Entre-Duex-Mers
- Graves de Vayres
- Loupiac
- Cote de Bordeaux-Saint-Macaire
- Sainte-Croix-du-Mount
- Sainte-Foy-Bordeaux
- Cotes de Bordeaux
- Premieres Cotes de Bordeaux
- Cote de Bourg
- Blaye/Cotes de Blaye

30 Kilometers / 18.6 Miles

Gironde Estuary

Libourne

Bordeaux

Dordogne River

Garonne River

Appellation system

Regional appellation

Bordeaux AOP is the largest appellation in the region, in size and production. Grapes can come from anywhere in the entire area.

Sub-Regional or District appellations

The highest appellations attainable in a particular locality, which may also group several village appellations, such as Haut-Médoc AOP and Entre-deux-Mers AOP.

Commune appellations

They are the smallest AOPs in each region and generally produce the highest quality wines. For example:

- **Pauillac, Saint-Estèphe, Saint Julien, Margaux, Pomerol, Saint-Émilion, Listrac-Médoc** and **Moulis-en-Médoc**.

The Châteaux Concept

Unlike Burgundy and many other French wine growing regions, most vineyards in Bordeaux are not associated with the name of their specific plots of land, but are instead known by the title of "Château". Although this word is a direct translation of "castle" (or manor house), not all Bordeaux Châteaux display the classic, conventional architecture of one. Rather than describing a specific vineyard location, this title operates as a brand for estates that exists under one single ownership.

In fact, the size of an estate may change over time along with the sale and/or purchase of vineyards and land in general. The Château Petrus in Pomeral, for instance, owns 50% more planted acres today than it did 50 years ago.

LEFT BANK

Médoc

The Médoc is Bordeaux's most acclaimed red wine growing region. Before becoming France's best Cabernet Sauvignon producer – and setting the standard for wines crafted from the same grape, worldwide - the area was, believe it or not, a gloomy, humid pine forest and salt marsh. Dutch engineers then drained the wetland in the 17th century, uncovering fertile beds of gravel and allowing now famed castles to be erected. The latter emerged as true emblems of Bordeaux wine.

Governors of the Dutch Wine merchants Guild, 17th century.

Dutch wine and spirits vats.

Location and geography

The Médoc is located to the North of the city of Bordeaux and lies along the Gironde estuary.

Soil composition

The region's soils are predominantly composed of gravel, which retains great moisture draining properties. Gravel is perfect for Cabernet Sauvignon production.

Grape varieties

Red
- Cabernet Sauvignon based blends.

Other grape varieties

- Cabernet Franc. Imparts herbal spice, red fruit, and tannins.
- Malbec. Can soften the austerity of Cabernet Sauvignon.
- Merlot. The mostly widely planted. Contributes a fleshly, juicy texture.
- Petit Verdot. Offers color, depth, and exotic perfume.
- Carménère.

Sub-region appellations of Médoc

- **Médoc AOP**
- **Haut-Médoc**

Village appellations

- **Saint-Estèphe AOP**
- **Pauillac AOP**
- **Saint-Julien AOP**
- **Margaux AOP**
- **Listrac-Médoc AOP**
- **Moulis-en-Médoc AOP**

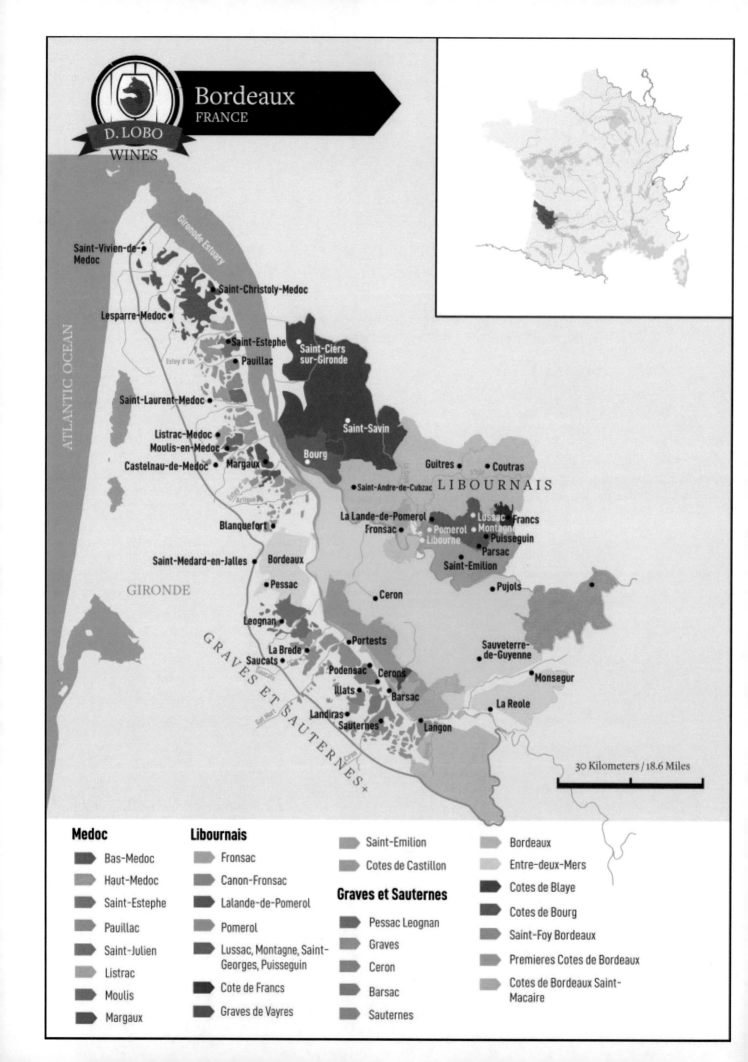

1855 Classification

A ranking of Bordeaux's top châteaux was commissioned by Emperor Napoleon III for the Universal Exposition held in Paris. Merchants and brokers came up with a ranking of 61 properties, divided in five tiers, from **first growth through fifth growth** (premier, second, troisième, quatrième and cinquième cru). To do so, they followed the **historical record of market prices** for each property's wines: **the higher the price, the higher the ranking**...

The Right Bank's communes were not part of this classification.
One property in the Pessac-Léognan commune in Graves, south of the Médoc, was included, Château Haut-Brion, after had a long fetched a very high price in the market.

.

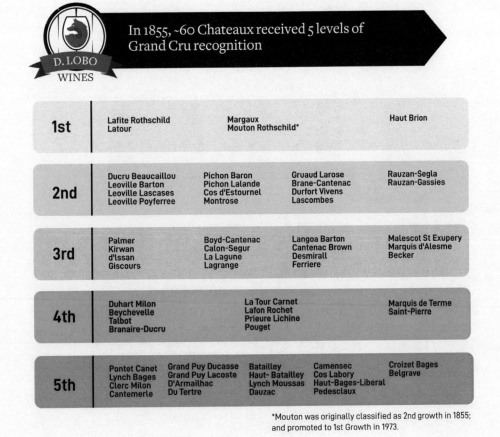

In 1855, ~60 Chateaux received 5 levels of Grand Cru recognition

D. LOBO WINES

1st	Lafite Rothschild Latour	Margaux Mouton Rothschild*		Haut Brion
2nd	Ducru Beaucaillou Leoville Barton Leoville Lascases Leoville Poyferree	Pichon Baron Pichon Lalande Cos d'Estournel Montrose	Gruaud Larose Brane-Cantenac Durfort Vivens Lascombes	Rauzan-Segla Rauzan-Gassies
3rd	Palmer Kirwan d'Issan Giscours	Boyd-Cantenac Calon-Segur La Lagune Lagrange	Langoa Barton Cantenac Brown Desmirail Ferriere	Malescot St Exupery Marquis d'Alesme Becker
4th	Duhart Milon Beychevelle Talbot Branaire-Ducru	La Tour Carnet Lafon Rochet Prieure Lichine Pouget		Marquis de Terme Saint-Pierre
5th	Pontet Canet Lynch Bages Clerc Milon Cantemerle	Grand Puy Ducasse Grand Puy Lacoste D'Armailhac Du Tertre	Batailley Haut- Batailley Lynch Moussas Dauzac	Camensec Cos Labory Haut-Bages-Liberal Pedesclaux	Croizet Bages Belgrave

*Mouton was originally classified as 2nd growth in 1855; and promoted to 1st Growth in 1973.

Two additional designations characterize quality Bordeaux Châteaux that were not included in the 1855 classification of crus classés (classed growths) - Cru Artisan and Cru Bourgeois:

- Cru Artisan, a designation that has been in use for nearly 150 years. In total, 36 small producers throughout the Médoc had the right to use the designation to indicate their outstanding winemaking expertise. Rankings are updated every five years.

- Some of these châteaux include Château Andron, Château Béjac Romelys, Château Haut-Brisey. Château Haut-Gravat, Château Vieux Gadet, Château de Coudot, Château Moutte Blanc, Château de Lagua, Château du Hâ, Château Lamongeau, Château Micalet, Château Linot, Château Graves de Pez and many others.

- Cru Bourgeois, designation first introduced in 1932. Dividing properties in three categories:

- Cru Bourgeois Exceptionnel
- Cru Bourgeois Supérieur
- Cru Bourgeois.

Top recent vintages of the Médoc

2005, 2009, 2010, and 2015.

First Growth of Bordeaux

Left Bank village appellations

- Saint-Estèphe AOP

As the northmost town appellation in Haut-Médoc. Saint-Estèphe produces sturdy, full-bodied reds. The commune does not host any first growths and is only home to five crus classés: Château Calon-Ségur, Château Cos d'Estournel, Château Cos Labory, Château Lafon-Rochet and Château Montrose.

- Pauillac AOP

As a classic claret, Pauillac flaunts three first growths: Château Mouton-Rothschild, Château Lafite and Château Latour, the last two being the pinnacle of Pauillac. While Latour produces strong, intense wines, Lafite displays elegance and aroma. The commune's gravel topsoil allows for its wines to taste complex and long lived.

- Saint-Julien AOP

Saint-Julien crafts less wine than its neighbors, but why would it matter? The rouge's quality is excellent and the style elegant. In fact, around 80% of the AOP's wines are crus classés. And though the commune hosts no first growths, it does have a great selection of five second growths: Château Léoville Barton, Château Léoville Las Cases, Château Léoville Poyferre, Château Gruaud-Larose, and Château Ducru-Beaucaillou.

- Margaux AOP

Being the largest commune appellation of the Haut-Médoc, Margaux AOP stretches throughout five villages: Arsac, Cantenac, Labarde, eponym Margaux and Soussans. It also has a bigger number of crus classés than any other town with an impressive list of 21, including Premier Cru Château Margaux and other crus, such as Château Brane-Cantenac, Château Ferrière, Château Giscours, Château d'Issan, Château Lascombes and Château Palmer to name a few. Often described as "feminine", these red wines display a fruity, exotic finesse like no other.

- Listrac-Médoc AOP

Do not let the Listrac-Médoc region fool you. Albeit cramped and small, its wines are deep and feature a long-lived and age-worthy character. Château Baudan, Château Donissan, Château Lafon and Château Martinho are among Listrac's best crus.

- Moulis-en-Médoc

Moulis-en-Médoc's wines are highly praised and many of them represent the best wines of Médoc - notably thanks to the Crus Bourgeois designation. You might have heard of some of its best properties, such as Château Antonic, Château Brillette, Château Chasse-Spleen and Château Pujeaux.

Graves

By the time Médoc's swampland became practicable, the wines of Graves had already been poured in the bronze chalice of King Charles II. It was Samuel Pepys, Chief Secretary to the Admiralty and famous diarist, who exported Graves wines onto English tables, and eulogized the excellence of delectable Château "Ho-Bryan" (Haut-Brion), in 1663. The latter was apparently sold under the name of "Aubrion", back in 1521, according to some 2014 Bordeaux archives. The very first traceable estate in the region, however, is Château Pape-Clément. As its name implies, the Domaine was owned by Pope Clément V, from 1305 to 1309 - the year he gifted the estate to Bordeaux.

Similar to the Médoc, Graves' sand, gravel and clay soil (also known as Boulbènes) becomes sandier towards the south. The Graves AOP appellation covers both rouge and dry white wines, which were first classified in 1953, for the exception of Premier Cru Château Haut-Brion. The commune currently hosts a total of 13 red and 9 white crus classés.

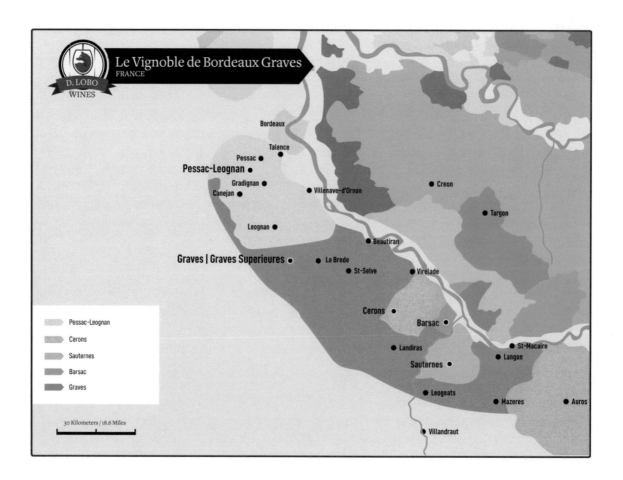

1959 Classification

The wines of Graves were ranked in 1953 by an Institut National des Appellations d'Origine appointed jury, then approved by the Minister of Agriculture in August of that same year. The selection was revised in February 1959 and a few additions were made. The classification covers both red and white wines. All châteaux belong to the appellation Pessac-Léognan, which eventually came into effect on September 9, 1987.

Crus Classés	Communes	Styles of wine
Château Bouscaut	Cadaujac	Red and white wine
Château Charbonnieux	Léognan	Red and white wine
Domaine de Chevalier	Léognan	Red and white wine
Château Latour-Martillac	Martillac	Red and white wine
Château Malartic-Lagravière	Léognan	Red and white wine
Château Olivier	Léognan	Red and white wine
Château de Fieuzal	Léognan	Red wine only
Château Haut-Bailly	Léognan	Red wine only
Château Haut-Brion	Pessac	Red wine only
Château La Mission Haut-Brion	Pessac	Red wine only
Château Pape Clément	Pessac	Red wine only
Château Smith Haut Lafite	Martillac	Red wine only
Château La Tour Haut-Brion	Talence	Red wine only
Château Couhins	Villanave d'Ornon	White wine only
Château Couhins Lurton	Léognan	White wine only
Château Laville Haut-Brion	Talence	White wine only

Graves appellations

Sub-region Pessac-Léognan AOP

First created in 1987, it became a prestige appellation for both red and dry white wines.

Communes

- Pessac
- Léognan
- Cadaujac
- Gradignan
- Marillac
- Merignac
- Talence
- Villenave-d'Ornon
- Saint-Médard-d'Eyrans

Graves Supérieur AOP. Sweet white wines from three smaller apppellations.

- Cérons
- Barsac
- Sauternes

Sauternes appellations

It is no wonder that the dessert wines of Sauternes rank among some of the world's costliest bottles. Crafted from Sémillon, Sauvignon Blanc and Muscadelle vines, Sauternes AOPs display an intense complexity and spiced sweetness with their interesting hints of honey, ginger and saffron. An engaging bouquet of flavors that is owed to Sauternes's unique climate and predisposition for the development of the noble Botrytis cinereal rot. When the latter attacks the grape, it proceeds to dehydrate the fruit, which allows sugar and acidity levels to take over and form that inherent spiced intricacy, impossible to duplicate through a normal dehydration process.

The wines of Sauternes were classified alongside the Médoc's in 1855, divided into premiers and seconds crus. One domaine, the Château d'Yquem, was ranked as a Premier Cru Supérieur for its legendary and highly esteemed liquory wines. During poor yielding years, like 1992 and 1974 for instance, the estate does not produce any wine. But during prolific years, Yquem will send its reapers out in the vineyards more than a dozen times if deemed necessary. The château is also known to craft one Bordeaux Supérieur, a dry white wine sold under the name of "Y" (pronounced Ee-grek).

Sauternes covers fives villages:

- **Sauternes**
- **Barsac** (The wines of Barsac may be sold as either Barsac AOP or Sauternes AOP)
- **Fargues**
- **Preignac**
- **Bommes**

Location and geography

The Left Bank is located south of Médoc and directly south and around the city of Bordeaux.

Soil composition

Gravel is the main component of Left Bank soils.

Grape varieties

White
- Sauvignon Blanc
- Sémillon

Red
- Cabernet Sauvignon
- Cabernet Franc
- Merlot

Sub-region appellations

- **Pessac-Léognan AOP**. Northernmost part of Graves. Dry white and red wines.
- **Sauternes AOP**. Southernmost part of Graves.

Vinification

A lot of Botrytis-affected sweet wines, mostly oaked aged in new French tonneaux are produced in the region.

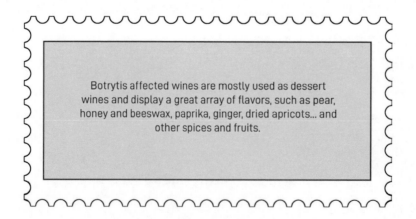

Botrytis affected wines are mostly used as dessert wines and display a great array of flavors, such as pear, honey and beeswax, paprika, ginger, dried apricots... and other spices and fruits.

Botrytis

Botrytis cinerea is a necrotrophic fungus that affects many plant species, although wine grapes are its most frequent hosts. In viticulture, this fungus is commonly known as "botrytis bunch rot" and in horticulture, it takes the names of "grey mould" in British English or "gray mold" in American English. The disease may cause two different types of infection on grapes. The first, grey rot, is the result of consistently wet conditions and typically destroys the affected clusters. The second, noble rot, occurs when drier conditions follow humidity and can result in distinctively sweeter dessert wines.

Stage 2 (S2)

Stage 3 (S3)

Entre-deux-Mers, Bourg and Côte-de-Bordeaux

Contrary to what one might think, the oldest vineyards in Bordeaux do not belong to the Médoc, or to the Right Bank of Dordogne. They are actually found in the smaller limestone hills of Bourg and Côtes-de-Bourg AOPs, first introduced to the art of viticulture by Roman conquerors. Bourg and Blaye, a neighboring town, produced well-acclaimed wines for centuries before Médoc and Graves wines stole the spotlight in the late 17th century. Today, Côtes-de-Bourg and Blaye AOP mainly produce red wines. Côtes-de-Blaye AOP, on the other hand, mostly crafts unique dry whites wines juiced from Ugni Blanc and Colombard vines.

However, many estates in the north corner of the Bordeaux region are now a part of the 2008 established Côtes-de-Bordeaux system. Indeed, a few appellations in the region are now labeled as Côtes-de-Bordeaux AOP in order to simplify designation language, but also to create an alternative to Bordeaux's pricey Grands Vins. The Côtes-de-Bordeaux wines, mostly red, may still list the name of the commune of origin on the bottle. The communes are:

- **Francs**
- **Castillon**
- **Blaye**
- **Cadillac**
- **Sainte-Foy**

In order to find sweet and fruity white wines, one will have to travel to the Garonne's eastern shore where the Cadillac, Loupiac and Sainte-Croix-du-Mont AOPs belong. The Premières Côtes-de-Bordeaux appellation also produces sweet wines, and drier or moelleux ones can be found in Côtes-de-Bordeaux Saint-Macaire, south of Loupiac, or in Entre-deux-Mers ("land between two seas"), one of Bordeaux's largest white wine producing region. Entre-deux-Mers may use the Haut-Benauge geographical designation, but its wines must remain dry.

.

Location and geography

Entre-deux-Mers translates to "land between two seas". This large area lies right between the Garonne and Dordogne rivers.

Soil composition

Very fertile silt.

Grape varieties

White
- Sauvignon Blanc
- Sémillon
- Muscadelle

Vinification

- Dry red and white wines, some sweet wines are produced in some AOPs.
- Little to no oak is used, stainless steel is preferred.
- Red wines made in this area fall under the Bordeaux AOP appellation.

Entre-deux-Mers appellations

- **Cadillac**
- **Loupiac**
- **Sainte-Croix-du-Mont**
- **Sainte-Foy**
- **Graves de Vayres**
- **Côtes de Bordeaux**
- **Haut-Bénauge**
- **Bergerac**

Entre-deux-Mers
FRANCE

D. LOBO
WINES

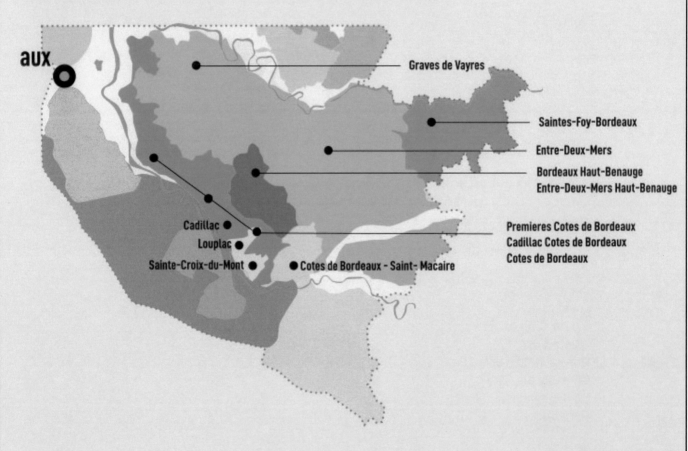

aux

Graves de Vayres

Saintes-Foy-Bordeaux

Entre-Deux-Mers

Bordeaux Haut-Benauge
Entre-Deux-Mers Haut-Benauge

Premieres Cotes de Bordeaux
Cadillac Cotes de Bordeaux
Cotes de Bordeaux

Cadillac
Louplac
Sainte-Croix-du-Mont
Cotes de Bordeaux - Saint- Macaire

RIGHT BANK

Just like Graves, the right bank of the Dordogne River had been cultivating vineyards long before the Médoc was drained by the Dutch. As a matter of fact, the area is home to Château Ausone, titled after 4th century poet Ausonius, who we mentioned earlier: a skilled Roman writer and known wine afficionado, that had possibly planted some vines at the namesake Domaine.

The now famed rouge producing communes of Saint-Émilion and Pomerol only gained Médoc-level popularity after World War II. Their wines are typically made from Merlot and Cabernet Franc, with only a tiny portion of them containing Cabernet Sauvignon, such as Saint-Émilion's Château Figeac for instance.

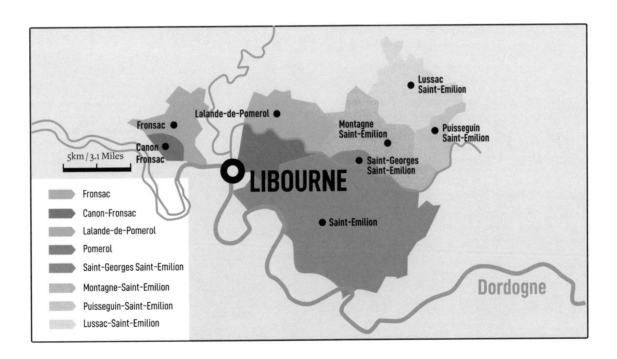

Saint-Émilion

In the 19th century, the Right Bank's wines only rarely made it overseas, unfortunately leading them to be excluded from the famous 1855 Classification. As a result, the commune of Saint-Émilion designed its own three-tier château ranking exactly one century later, with several revisions made in 1969, 1985, 1996, 2006 and last but not least, 2012. Evidently, this classification was intended to be revised about every decade, updating the rankings based on peer-reviewed wine tasting. However, demoted châteaux from the 2006 revision revolted against the jury's decision and dragged the issue in court. In 2009, Saint-Émilion agreed to allow promoted estates to stay in the rankings while ignoring any demotions. Moreover, a more generous "peace offering" classification, conducted by the INAO rather than local producers, was created in 2012.

It also important to note that, albeit a tad misleading, the Saint-Émilion Grand Cru AOP is an appellation, and not a classification. Wines labeled under that Grand Cru appellation – like all Grand Crus Classés wines without exception - must display 0.5% more alcohol than a simple Saint-Émilion AOP, and are required to undergo a longer period of élevage, the progression of wines between fermentation and bottling.

Location and geography

Saint-Émilion is located along the Dordogne River, near the town of Libourne.

Soil composition

The region forms a large bed of silt, clay, sand, limestone plateau and gravel.

Grape varieties

Red
- Merlot
- Cabernet Franc

Saint-Émilion appellations

- Saint-Émilion AOP
- Saint-Émilion Grand Cru AOP

An appellation, not a classification. Wines must have an additional 0.5% alcohol and must undergo a longer aging than wines labeled Saint-Émilion AOP. Red wines only.

Saint-Émilion satellites

- Lussac
- Saint-Georges
- Montagne
- Puisseguin

Classification system

Instituted in 1955, with a goal of revision every 10 years, the most recent revision was in 2012.

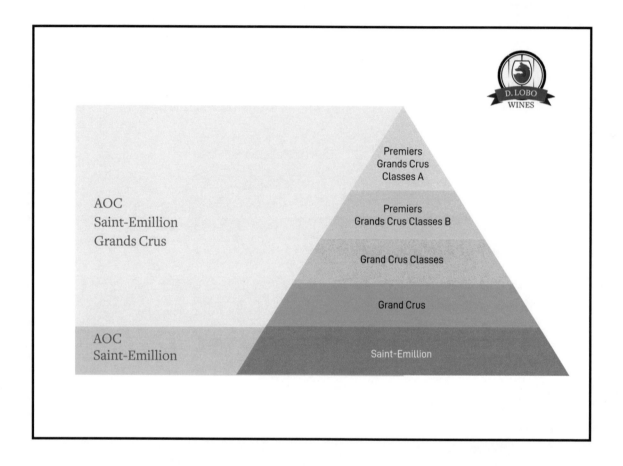

Some Saint-Émilion producers

- **Château Fombrauge**
- **Château Laroque**
- **Château Troplong Mondot**
- **Château La Dominique**

Premier Grands Crus Classés A

- Ausone
- Angelus
- Château Cheval-Blanc
- Château Pavie

Premier Grands Crus Classés B

14 named châteaux:

Château Beauséjour, Château Canon, Clos Fourtet, La Mondotte, Château Trotte Vieille, Château Beau-Séjour Bécot, Château Canon-la-Gaffelière, Château Pavie-Macquin, Château Valandraud, Château Bélair-Monange, Château Figeac, Château Larcis Ducasse, Château Troplong Mondot.

Grands Crus Classés

64 named châteaux:

Château L'Arrosée, Château Bellefont-Belcier, Château Cadet Bon, Château Clos de Sarpe, Château Corbin, Château Faugères, Château Fleur Cardinale, Château Fonplegade, Château Grand Corbin, Château Les Grandes Murailles, Château Haut-Sarpe, Château Jean Faure, Château La Roque, Château La Marzelle, Clos d'Oratoire, Château Petit Faurie de Soutard, Château Quinault L'Enclos, Château Saint-Georges, Château La Serre, Château La Tour Figeac, Château Bellevue, Château Guadet, Château Balestard La Tonnelle, Château Cap de Mourlin, Château La Clotte, Château de Beaulieu, Château Destieux, Château Faurie de Souchard, Château La Fleur Morange, Château Fonroque, Château Grand Corbin-Despagne, Château Grand Pontet, Clos des Jacobins, Château Laniote, Château Laroze, Château Monbousquet, Château Pavie-Decesse, Château de Pressac, Château Ripeau, Clos Saint-Martin, Château Soutard, Château Villemaurine, Château Barde-Haut, Château Berliquet, Château Chauvin, Château La Commanderie, Château La Couspaude, Château La Dominique, Château de Ferrand, Château Fombrauge, Château Franc Mayne, Château Grand Mayne, Couvent des Jacobins, Château Larmande, Clos la Madeleine, Château Moulin du Cadet, Château, Château Péby Faugères, Château Le Prieuré, Château Rochebelle, Château Sansonnet, Château Tertre Daugay, Château Yon Figeac.

Pomerol

With its five square miles and exactly 800 hectares (1,975 acres) of vineyards, Pomerol is on the smaller side compared to other AOPs, and the commune hosts not one cru classé. Regardless, its best châteaux – Château Lafleur, Château Pétrus, Château Le Pin, Château Trotanoy and Vieux-Château-Certan – are often sold at premiers crus prices ! Smaller wine lands seem to offer real treasures...

As a matter of fact, little Pomerol was one of Bordeaux's trendsetters, as a new and unofficial designation appeared in the late 1900s: the "microchâteau", also known as the garagistes movement. All it took was only a handful of acres for Pomerol's Le Pin as well as Château Valandraud and La Mondotte in Saint-Émilion, among others, to craft impressively ripe and structured wines. To put it into perspective, Château Latour manufactures between 150,000 and 180,000 bottles a year, but Le Pin only makes around 6,000. It is not a secret: rarity makes more money, and microchâteaux wines are no exception. Although their prices have somewhat dropped in recent years, the most esteemed ones still maintain extravagant rates.

© Jeff Leve, publisher and wine writer for The Wine Cellar Insider
www.thewinecellarinsider.com

Location and geography

Along the Dordogne River near the town of Libourne to the northwest of Saint-Émilion.

Soil composition

Sand, clay, gravel, and a subsoil of iron pan and rich clay.

Grape varieties

Red
- Merlot and Cabernet Fran based blends.

Pomerol appellations

- **Fronsac AOP**
- **Canon-Fronsac**
- **Lalande-de-Pomerol AOP**, which contains two communes:

- **Lalande-de-Pomerol**
- **Néac**

Pomerol wines

Highly-esteemed by wine enthusiats all around the world, the red appellation of Pomerol stands out from other Bordeaux designations by being a premium rouge producer without conforming to the region's châteaux and classifiation systems.

A GLANCE AT CHAMPAGNE

Historical background

According to archeologists, the history of Champagne and its marvels begins 70 million years ago, with the Mesozoic era. At that time, northern France, along with Britain, were far from being the advanced territories we currently know of, as they were full submerged. The Earth then worked its geologic magic, and the seas receded, leaving behind them an impressive legacy of fossils, shells and minerals like limestone, for instance. Today, those marine remains can be found on the walls of Champagne's exceptional deep caves, and may possibly have impacted the flavor of the local effervescent wines.

With a clear passion for the art of viticulture, Roman conquerors are believed to be the first to introduce wine growing in the region, although its first recorded vineyard, Saint-Rémi's, dates back to the 5th century. The very name of Champagne comes from the Latin term "campania", which hints to the hills of the Italian province of Campania, south of Rome. But along with its lush, timbered vine growing hills – also known as La Champagne Viticole -, the region also features a contrastingly chalky and arid plateau – La Champagne Pouilleuse.

Interestingly enough, the region's wines were not known as namesake "Champagne" or vin de Champagne for most of the region's early history. Instead, they were sold as "vins de Reims", the capital city of Champagne, and "vins de la Rivière" in reference to the Marne river, one of the main wine trading routes, connecting the region to Paris. One other road, going from east to west, linked France's capital to western Germany and the last one, from north to south, paved the way from northern Belgium (Flanders) to Switzerland.

The other two were a road linking France's capital and western. Together, those three arteries allowed Champagne's wines to become the world-wide esteemed product it is today, but its strategic location also gave rise to a few armed conflicts and various settlements...

The incredible Crayères of Champagne

After settling in Gaul, the Romans were in dire need of stone to build the ancient city of Reims. They thus decided to dig three hundred 40-meter (120 feet) deep chambers – no less - in Champagne's chalky ground. Also known as Crayères, these immense, cold, dark and eerily quiet chalk pits are now used by Champagne estates to age their wines, and are one of Reims's most impressive attractions...

Molded like pyramids – the deepest parts being the widest and the tops being narrow to limit air exposure and keep the chalk moist and easy to carve out –; the humid but sturdy Crayères are considered a true miracle of construction, as one could wonder how their engineering was even made possible in the first place.

During World War I, the Crayères became home to 20,000 refugees, who lived down in the quarries' depth and soundness for years after Reims was bombed. As a matter of fact, Veuve Clicquot and Ruinart's chalk pits used to serve as makeshift hospitals, and stopgap school classes were laid out in Pommery's.

Historical figures of Champagne

Dom Pérignon

Dom Pierre Pérignon was a 17th century Benedictine monk and is praised to be the "Father of Champagne". Dom Pérignon is known to have created the golden rules of Champagne making, as his focus was to produce wines of top quality and to make the clearest Champagne from red grapes. Along with introducing the cork system in France after seeing it in Spain, he thought of more effective vine growing and training techniques, and current wine growers and enthusiasts still credit him for the art of blending. Moreover, the aging techniques that he put in place in the 1600s are still used up to this day..

Louis XV

Also known as Louis the Beloved, Louis XV was the King of France from 1715 until his death in 1774. Under his rule, all Champagne bottles had to be the same shape and size, for uniformity purposes as well as to make the product stand out from other wines. The bottles' corks had to be tied down, plugged in the bottle's mouth and attached with the wiry string we know of and use today. Moreover, Champagne had to be shipped and distributed directly in bottles rather than in the traditional wood barrels.

Veuve Clicquot

In 1805, young widow Barbe Nicole Clicquot inherited her deceased husband's Champagne domaine. Famously known as "Veuve Clicquot" (the Clicquot widow) and additionally baptized "grande dame de la Champagne", she became the first woman to manage a Champagne house, and one of the first business women of her time, at only 27 years old. Madame Cliquot is also praised for having invented the remuage technique (riddling), helping other winemakers with settlement.

The English influence in Champagne

The British, who already were known wine enthousiasts by the 17th century, were among the first to praise Champagne's effervescence and to try understanding where the sparkling came from. According to scientist Christopher Merret, who released the first report on the matter in 1662, the presence of sugar is the main cause of effervescence in wines. In fact, his paper detailed how adding sugar to almost any wine before bottling them could cause them to sparkle, and hints today that the British were producing sparkling Champagne even before the French... By the end of the 1600s, glass making was already well advanced in Britain thanks to the works of acclaimed George Ravenscroft and others. The country was manufacturing thicker and sturdier bottles that could contain bubbly wines without exploding, and as their glass blowing techniques improved, the popularity of sparkling Champagne took off.

Location and geography

The Champagne region is located in northern France, about 90 miles northeast of Paris.

Climate

The region's climate can be described as cool continental and unfortunately has no natural protection from the Atlantic winds and cloudy, unpredictable weather. Champagne is one of the coolest wine growing regions in the world.

Soil composition

Limestone and chalk are the main components of the region's soils. Vine roots make their way deep in these grounds, which provide drainage while retaining moisture. The soils maintain a fairly constant temperature throughout the year.

Grape varieties

White
- Chardonnay. Chardonnay provides elegance and longevity.

Red
- Pinot Noir. Pinot Noir supports the wine's structure, richness, and body.
- Meunier. Pinot Meunier lends a youthful fruitiness and approachability.

Other grapes permitted in Champagne

- Pinot Blanc
- Arbanne
- Fromenteau
- Petit Meslier

Viticulture

The northern location means that growers in Champagne face persistent of rain, frost, and hail.

Vinification

- Most Champagne is a blend of grapes (Chardonnay, Pinot Noir, and Pinot Meunier).
- Sub-regions, villages, and vineyards.
- Vintages

The wines of Champagne are made thanks to the Méthode Champenoise, also known as the méthode classique if used to make non-Champagne sparkling wines. Regional wine laws help protect and regulate this specific method. All wines labeled Champagne must be sparkling and must use this method.

Méthode Champenoise

Step One. Making the base still wine

Grapes are pressed quickly and gently to avoid retaining color from the skins of the red grape varieties and to prevent oxidation. The base wine is very light in color, low in alcohol and high acidity. Fermentation can occur in either stainless-steel tanks or oak barrels.

Step Two. Assemblage of the "cuvée" - Assembling the blend

Champagne can be a blend of grapes, vintages (seen on the label non-vintage), region, villages, or vineyards. The blend is made at this early stage.

Step Three. Secondary fermentation. Creating the bubbles

The base wine is then bottled with a syrupy mixture of yeast and sugar, called the **liqueur de tirage**. The bottle is sealed with a crown cap and, over time, the yeast metabolizes the sugar, creating a small amount of alcohol and carbon dioxide (CO_2) gas. The CO_2 is trapped in the bottle and creates the bubbles.

Step Four. Sur Lie Aging

After the liqueur de tirage has induced the secondary fermentation, the yeast cells gradually break down this is called **autolysis**. The wine is rested on the lees in the bottle (**sur lie aging**). By law, all Champagne must spend at least 12 months on the lees as part of the minimum 15 months of total aging required. Sur lie aging imparts aromas and flavors reminiscent of yeast, dough, and fresh baked bread.

Step Five. **Remuage** – Riddling. Removal of sediment (part 1)

After aging, the lees must be removed from the bottle in order to have a clear wine. Each bottle is gently turned to gradually move the lees into its neck. This can be done by hand or by machine.

By hand. A **pupitre** is a wooden A-frame wine rack. It was first created by **Madame Clicquot** known as the **"Grande Dame of Champagne"**. The rack holds 60 bottles, each of which is hand-turned. This process takes about 8 weeks to complete.

By machine. A **gyropalette** is a large machine that can hold 505 bottles at a time. It takes

Step Six. **Dégorgement** – Disgorging. Removal of sediment (part 2)

Once the sediment has collected in the neck of the bottle, it needs to be removed. To disgorge the sediment, each bottle's neck is frozen in an ice bath, so that the yeast can be ejected. This can be done by hand or, as is more often the case, by machine.

Step Seven. **Dosage**

After dégorgement, a mixture of wine and sugar called the **liqueur d'expédition** is added to the bottle. The amount of sugar added determines the sweetness level and, therefore, the style of the Champagne.

D. LOBO
WINES

Methode Champenoise

Harvest
(Pinot Noir,
Pinot Meunler
Chardonnay)

Grapes for champagne are harvested early, when they have high acid levels and low sugar levels.

1st
Fermentation

This step creates a still, dry, low alcohol wine. Each grape variety is usually fermented individually.

Blending
(*Assemblage*)

These still, dry, varietal wines are blended into the house style. Usually, this includes wines from several different years.

2nd
Fermentation

The liqueur de tirage (a combination of yeast and sugar) is added to the blend to start a 2nd fermentation *in the bottle*. This makes the bubbles!

Maturation
(Tirage)

After the fermentation is complete, the wine is left to mature in contact with the dead yeast cells. The yeast gives toasty, bready aromas to the wine. By law, Champagne must mature in this way for at least 12 months.

Riddling
(*Remuage*)

After maturation, the yeast must be removed from the bottle, or the wine will be cloudy. The bottles are slowly rotated untill they are upside down, with the yeast in the neck of the bottle.

Disgorgement
(*Degorgement*)

Once the bottles are upside down with the yeast in the neck, the necks of the bottles are frozen, the caps romved, and the pressure in the bottle shoots out the frozen plug of wine with the yeast inside.

Dosage

Since disgorgement leaves the bottle less than full, some wine is added to fill up the space. This wine, the *dosage*, will usually have some amount of sugar added to it. This determines the final sweetness level of the Champagne

Corking

The final product will contain 6 atmospheres of pressure - as much as a car tire!

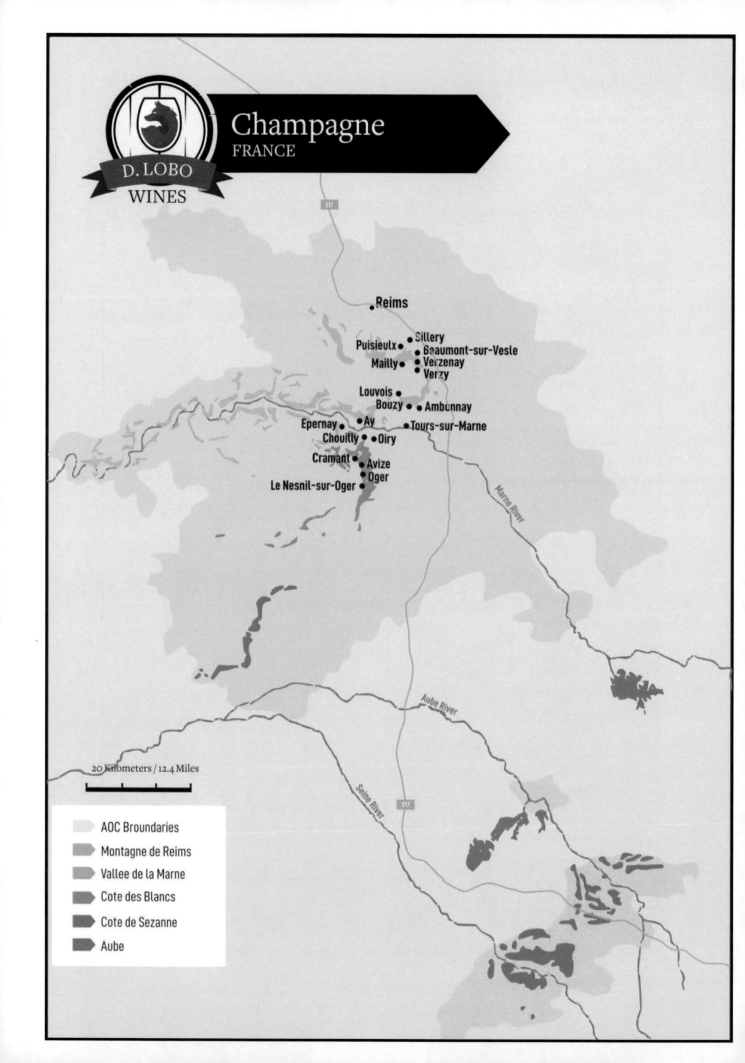

Champagne sweetness levels, style categories and bottle sizes

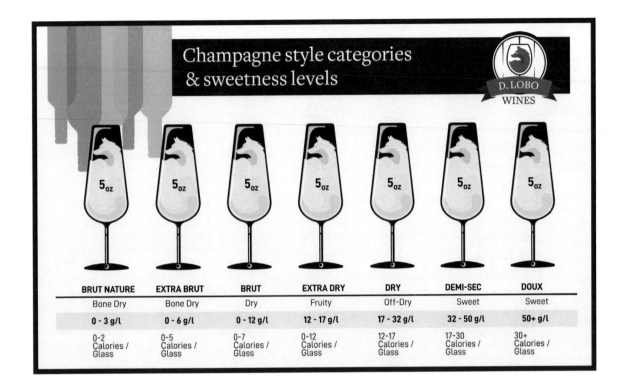

Champagne AOP

Sparkling wine made with Méthode Champenoise.

Champagne sub-regions

- **Valle de la Marne.** Meunier is the prominent grape.
- **Côte des Blancs.** Chardonnay is the prominent grape.
- **Montagne de Reims.** Pinot Noir is the prominent grape.
- **Côte de Sézanne.** Chardonnay is the prominent grape.
- **Côte des Bars (The Aube).** Pinot Noir is the prominent grape.

Grand Cru villages of Champagne. There is a total of 17 Grand Cru Villages in Champagne.

- **Montagne de Reims**
    - **Ambonnay**
    - **Beaumont-sur-Vesle**
    - **Bouzy**
    - **Louvois**
    - **Mailly-Champagne**
    - **Puisieulx**
    - **Sillery**
    - **Verzenay**
    - **Verzy**

- **Côte des Blancs**
    - **Avize**
    - **Chouilly**
    - **Cramant**
    - **Le Mesnil-sur-Oger**
    - **Oger**
    - **Oiry**

- **Vallée de la Marne**
    - **Ay**
    - **Tours-sur-Marne**

Premier Cru villages. There is a total of 44 Pemier Cru villages in Champagne.

Avenay, Bergères-lès-Vertus, Bezannes, Billy le Grand, Bisseuil, Chamery, Champillon, Chigny-les-Roses, Chouilly (PN), Coligny (CH), Cormontreuil, Coulommes la Montagne, Cuis, Cumières, Dizy, Écueil, Étréchy (CH), Grauves, Hautvillers, Jouy les Reims, Les Mesneux, Ludes, Mareuil-sur-Ay, Montbré, Mutigny, Pargny-lès-Reims, Pierry, Rilly-la-Montagne, Sacy, Sermiers, Taissy, Tauxières, Tours-sur-Marne (CH), Trépail, Trois Puits, Vaudemanges, Vertus, Villedommange, Villeneuve-Renneville, Villers-Allerand, Villers-aux-Noeuds, Villers-Marmery, Voipreux and Vrigny.

Some Champagne producers

Light, elegant styles

- **Billecart-Salmon**
- **Laurent-Perrier**
- **Perrier-Jouet**
- **Ruinart**

Medium-bodied styles

- **Alfred Gratien**
- **Lanson**
- **Moet & Chandon**
- **Taittinger**

Full-bodied styles

- **Bollinger**
- **Gosset**
- **Louis Roeder**
- **Krug**
- **Salon**

Types of Champagne producers

Every bottle of Champagne bears a matriculation number - a code that is assigned to every producer by the CIVC. This number is made of a series of digits, preceded by a set of initials that indicate the type of producer.

- **NM (Négociant Manipulant)**: An estate that buys grapes and/or base wines from growers and smaller houses. Some NM houses own most of their vineyards while others do not. Although quality varies widely, prices remain uniformly high.

- **RM (Récoltant Manipulant)**: A grower-producer who makes Champagne predominantly from their own harvests - 95% of the grapes must originate from the producer's own estate.

- **CM (Coopérative Manipulant)**: A growers' co-operative that produces wine under one single brand.

- **RC (Récoltant Coopérateur)**: A grower whose grapes are vinified at a co-operative, but sells end-product under their own label.

- **SR (Société de Récoltants)**: A firm (not a co-operative) inaugurated by a union of growers (often related) who share resources to make their wines and collectively market several brands.

- **ND (Négociant Distributeur)**: A middleman company that distributes Champagne it did not make.

- **MA (Marque d'Acheteur)**: A buyer's own brand, often a large supermarket chain or restaurant, that purchases Champagne and sells it under its own label.

Champagne age designations

- **Non-vintage (NV)**. Aged minimum of 15 months, with at least 12 months spent on lees. Any Champagne without a vintage year on the label is only the basic style of Champagne, and wine produced from 3 or more harvests usually makes a non-vintage blend. These wines may also be made of base wines originating from 30 or 40 different villages.

- **Vintage Champagne**. Aged for a minimum of 36 months. Vintage Champagne is made entirely from the grapes that were harvested in a single year. It is therefore more intense in flavor, fuller-bodied and more complex than non-vintage Champagne.

The CIVC and Échelle des Crus

The CIVC is the regulatory body responsible for mediating relations between growers and producers. It supervises the production methods and promotion of Champagne and regulates the size of harvests, authorizes blocage and déblocage (the reserve and release of wine stocks for use in future vintages) and makes sure to preserve the protected designation of Champagne. Until 1985 - when a revision set the minimum rating of the scale at 80 -, the CIVC set the price of grapes based on the Échelle des Crus ("scale of crus) a percentile system by which the Champagne appellation villages or crus are rated, from 0 to 100. Villages that reached the top of the échelle (100) were classified as grands crus; villages that achieved an échelle of 90 through 99 were ranked as premiers crus. Mareuil-sur-Ay in the Vallée de la Marne and Tauxières in Montagne de Reims were the only premier cru villages with a 99% ranking. Villages with a rating below 90 were simply classified as crus.

Until 1990, a village's échelle rating represented the set price percentage that was allocated to a grower for their fruit, which meant that wine growers in grand cru villages would receive the full price set by the CIVC and other villages would receive the percentage equivalent to their own rating. Today, the CIVC oversees trade between growers and Champagne houses in order to promote fairness, rather than regulating prices. In the early 2000s, the CIVC abolished the Échelle de Crus system for good, but the premier and grand cru villages retain their titles and may continue to label their wines as such.

Champagne styles

- **Rosé.** A pink-colored Champagne made with 100% Pinot Noir grapes.
- **Blanc de Blancs**. 100% made with Chardonnay grapes.
- **Blanc de Noirs**. Champagne made with only the dark grapes Pinot Noir and Pinot Meunier.

Special cuvées and other bottlings

- **Single vineyard**. A noted single vineyard on the label.
- **Clos** or **Mono Parcel**. A noted single parcel in a vineyard under a single ownership.
- **Cuvée prestige** or **Tête de cuvée**. The top-end bottling of a particular Champagne house or producer

Vintage variations

- Huge weather extremes result in wide vintages as quality varies from season to season and year to year.
- There are a limited number of vintage wines in a decade.
- Most Champagnes are non-vintage wines.

For your culture

A year in Champagne, 2014. A movie by David Kennard

Top recent vintage of Champagne

- **2002.** The first great vintage of the decade. That year enjoyed a perfectly warm season and led to the growth of powerful, structured Pinot Noir grapes and luscious Chardonnays. Some wines show a tendency to corpulence: the best, released later, are superb and good for another 10 to 20 years.

- **2005**. A very productive harvest of healthy, quality grapes, especially white wines. That year gave birth to wines to enjoy between 2015 and 2020 or even later.

- **2008**. One of the best two vintages of this decade. Cooler in climate, that year led to the return of a classic dry style, perfectly balancing strong fruit and stimulating acidity. Best to consumer around 2025 or later.

- **2012**. That year's sunny August and warm September let to a small but spectacular Pinot Noir crop, often deemed to be as great as 1952's vintage. Wines from that year were to put on your shopping list in 2019 and 2020.

For your culture

Champagne Journal, 2014-2016, by wineunites on YouTube

This image represents the Moulin de Verzenay and Maison Mumm, two of Champagne's classified historic monuments.

A GLANCE AT THE LOIRE VALLEY

Historical Background

Flowing 630 miles from the Massif Central mountains to the Atlantic Coast, the Loire is France's longest river and is the last wild, untouched stream in Europe. The royal river is also known to irrigate some of the most esteemed wine appellations in the country. In fact, the Loire Valley's best vineyards form a near perfect ribbon from the Pays Nantais, which feeds off the Atlantic Ocean, to the Central Vineyards of the Upper Loire, which happen to be located at the exact center of France! Lucky enough to be nurtured by the eponym stream, the Loire Valley has been baptized "Jardin de France" (the garden of France), as it displays a beautiful, colorful combination of vineyards, other agricultural fields and diverse forests. The area is also known for its rich culture and history.

The Loire Valley, like many other wine growing regions in France, has been home to quality crus for many centuries. The first traces of winemaking in the area are believed to date back to at least the 1st century. In the eastern are of Touraine, viticulture was brought in the 500s, and the first Chenin Blanc grapes seem to have appeared around 845 in a few Anjou vineyards, although conclusive evidence of that does not arrive until the 16th century.

According to a publication written by French writer François Rabelais in 1534, the Cabernet Franc grape arrived in Loire vineyards around the same time as Chenin Blanc. However, it might have made its appearance in Western France as early as the 11th century, coming all the way from the Basque region. Either way, Loire wines like Sancerre, Anjou and Saint-Pourçain have always been an important part of France's culture and terroir and have existed on the menus of Parisian cafés for a long time. In fact, the wines crafted in the Valley had already gained fame during the Middle Ages, since the whole region was the focus of French society.

The public interest then shifted from the Loire Valley onto Paris and Louis XIV's Versailles, as the Industrial Age peeked and brought new wines, like Bordeaux's for instance, to Paris. What did not help was also the presence of phylloxera in Loire's vineyards, a devastating insect pest that raged in the 1880's and gravely affected the region's crops, leading the whole area to nearly sink into oblivion. Today, the Loire is fortunately back on track and offers an eclectic array of food-friendly wines, lighter in style than many of the best wines, but incredibly charming and authentic to the region.

More white wines are produced in the Loire Valley than in any other French region, and the area is second only to Champagne in bubbly wine production. Loire's classic and renowned varietal grapes for white wines include Chenin Blanc, Sauvignon Blanc and Melon de Bourgogne. The valley is also home to the Chardonnay, Chasselas, Gros Plant (Folle Blanche), Orbois (Arbois/Menu Pineau) and Romorantin regional and international grape varieties.

And while the Loire's white wines tend to overshadow the reds, the Valley stays an important source for lighter-bodied, high acid red wines:

- Cabernet Franc, known locally as Breton, is the most important varietal.
- Pinot Noir
- Gamay
- Cabernet Sauvignon
- Malbec (Côt)
- Pineau d'Aunis
- Groslot (Grolleau)

Loire Valley sub-regions:

- **Pays Nantais**
- **Anjou-Saumur**
- **Touraine**
- **Central Vineyards**

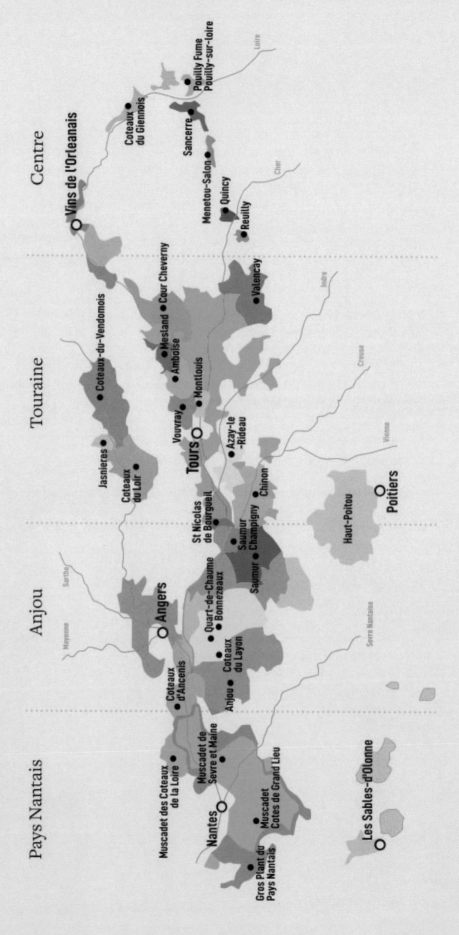

Pays Nantais

The vineyards of the Pays Nantais, also known as the Muscadet country expands from the south towards the northeast of Nantes and are exposed year-round to the cool but strong winds of the Atlantic – a perfect climate for the Melon de Bourgogne grape to thrive.
Appearing in the area in the 1600s a distiller's grains for the Dutch, the Melon the Bourgogne variety rose to fame after the 1709 frost that put the production of red wines on hold, leading the Pays Nantais to become a light and fresh white wine region instead. The grape is known under four different appellations: Muscadet AOP, Muscadet-Côtes-de-Grandlieu AOP, Muscadet-Côteaux-de-la-Loire AOP and Muscadet Sèvre-et-Maine AOP, all best at 12 % ABV or below.

Although Muscadet AOP is the basic appellation for the grape, it is rarely used since most producers are usually indicated to use one of the other three sub-labels. Muscadet AOP wines are high-acidity, go from bone dry to dry and are crafted for youthful consumption.
Created in 1994, the Muscadet-Côtes-de-Grandlieu appellation is the newest of all four, and the wines of this AOP still struggle to reach greater quality than a simple Muscadet. Muscadet-Côteaux-de-la-Loire AOP, on the other hand, provides excellent grapes and leaner, more flavorful wines.

As for Muscadet Sèvre-et-Maine AOP, which represents over 80% of overall Muscadet production, its wines are known to be age-worthy and producers like Guy Bossard are attempting to create a badge of quality to differentiate their wines and indicate their excellence. Some of them are already labeling their bottles with the "Hermine d'Or" mention, an unofficial designation that promotes terroir and age-ability of their wines. Muscadet Sèvre-et-Maine AOP wines come from 23 different communes, all located between the Sèvre and Maine rivers, offer a classic Melon de Bourgogne grown on quality soils like gneiss, silica, clay and granite, and half of them are bottled sur lie.

In order to raise the status of Muscadet Sèvre-et-Maine wines, a Cru Communaux designation was actually proposed in 2001. The motion required eligible wines from specified schist soils to spend a minimum of 18 months sur lie, longer than the actual sur lie term allows. It then took 10 years to finally see some results, with the introduction of three subzones for the appellation: Clisson, Le Pallet, and Gorges. Another four - Château-Thébaud, Goulaine, Monnières-Saint-Fiacre and Mouzillon-Tillières - were added more recently, in 2019. Wines from these villages and crus are expected to become some of the finest available, even if their minimum length of aging rules out the use of sur lie on the label.

2011 also marked the elimination of the Vin Délimité de Qualité Supérieure (VDQS) tier, and three new regions in Pays Nantais – Gros Plant du Pays Nantais, Côteaux d'Ancenis and the Fiefs Vendéens – gained AOC status. The first one on the list, Gros Plant du Pays Nantais, can be produced as a sur lie wine, although the area's producers might have to work a tad harder to improve perceptions.

A Muscadet wine must originate from one of the lands that qualify for one of the three sub-appellations in order to be labeled as sur lie. Sur lie wines are aged on their lees over the winter and are bottled directly off the fine lees, between March 1st and November 30th of the year following the harvest. This process is appreciated among producers for the intensity, complexity and slight sparkle it adds to their wines.

Lees aging

During the Lees aging process, white and effervescent wines are left to mature in contact with yeast responsible for the fermentation. Little by little, yeast cells die, which allows for nutty and flowery aromas to be release into the wine, rendering creamy and rich liquor-like bottles.

Location and geography

The Pays Nantais is located on the beautiful Atlantic Coast.

Climate

The climate is cool and wet maritime, since affected by being situated close to the Atlantic Ocean.

Soil composition

Gravel and sand over schist and granite are the main components of the region's soils.

Grape varieties

- Melon de Bourgogne
- Gros Plant (Folle Blanche)

Vinification

Sur lie aging. This term refers to the technique of aging wines on the remains of post-fermentation yeast cells (or "lees") to add complexity and richness to the finished wine.

Pays Nantais appellations

- **Muscadet AOP**
- **Muscadet Coteaux de la Loire AOP**
- **Muscadet Cotes de Grandlieu AOP**
- **Muscadet Sevre-et-Maine AOP**

Village appellations

- **Clisson**
- **Le Pallet**
- **Gorges**

AOCs

- **Gros Plant du Pays Nantais**
- **Côteaux d'Ancenis**
- **Fiefs Vendées**

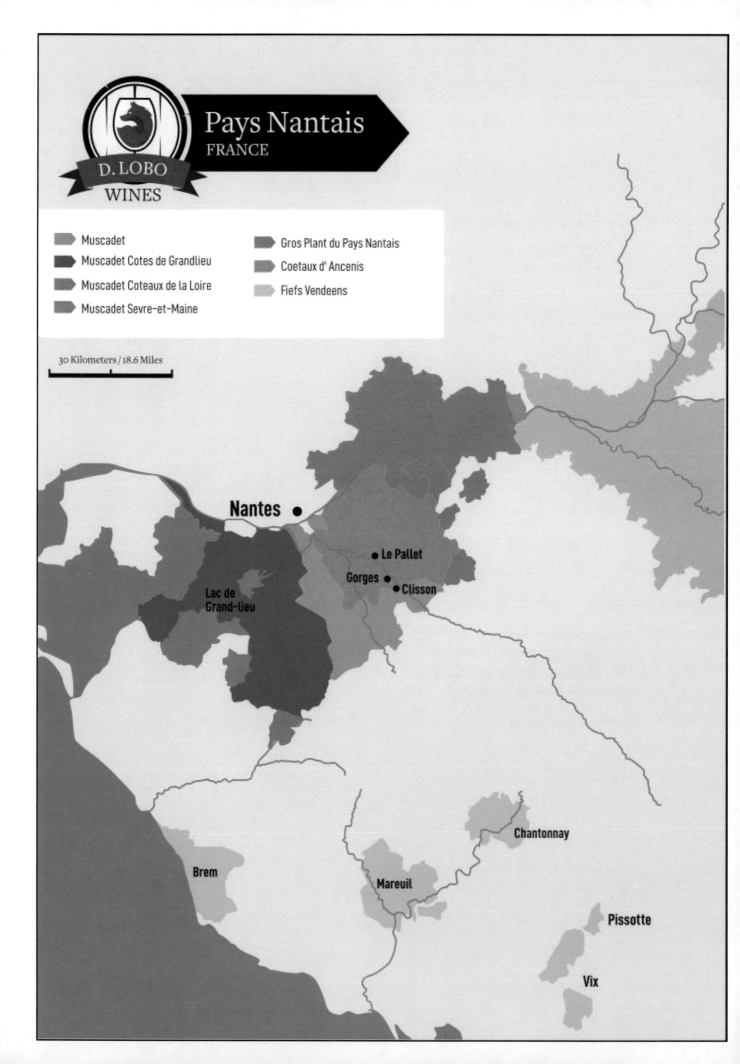

Pays Nantais
FRANCE

D. LOBO
WINES

Muscadet

Muscadet Cotes de Grandlieu

Muscadet Coteaux de la Loire

Muscadet Sevre-et-Maine

Gros Plant du Pays Nantais

Coetaux d' Ancenis

Fiefs Vendeens

30 Kilometers / 18.6 Miles

Nantes

Le Pallet

Gorges

Clisson

Lac de
Grand-lieu

Chantonnay

Brem

Mareuil

Pissotte

Vix

Anjou-Saumur

Anjou is the largest and most diverse region of the Loire. Located right between Pays Nantais and Touraine, it is often associated with its eastern neighbor, the subregion of Saumur. Collectively, both sub-regions produce all the styles of wines that can be found in the Loire valley.

Anjou

Although 45% of Anjou's turnout is devoted to rosé wines, the region is mostly known and esteemed for its excellent expressions of the Chenin Blanc grape – locally known as Pineau de la Loire. These golden white wines are often crafted to be sweet or dry. Anjou is also praised for its quality reds, as around 30% of the area's vineyards carry the delicious Cabernet Franc grape variety. The region's global appellation is Anjou AOP, a label that can be found on both Anjou and Saumur's red, white and sparkling wine bottles. Anjou wines, however, are never to be bottled as Saumur AOP.

Slow to ripen in Anjou's northerly climates, the Chenin Blanc grape generally keeps its high acidity, bitterness and astringent taste in the finished Anjou Blanc AOP wines. Contrastingly, Savennières AOP's dry wines – produced with 100% Chenin Blanc – are austere in their youth but develop a great complexity and a rich honey texture as they age. Located north of the Loire river, the Savennières vineyards benefit from great southern sun exposure and were planted on a unique soil blend of blue schist and volcanic debris. In 2011, the unofficial grands crus Roche Aux Moines and Coulée de Serrant finally achieved AOC status – Coulée de Serrant being a monopole of the excellent rigid and biodynamic Nicolas Joly wine.

Opposite to Savennières and south of the Loire, the producers of Côteaux du Layon AOP and Côteaux de l'Aubance AOP trigger their Chenin Blanc harvest a bit later in the season, in hopes that the noble rot, botrytis, will affect their crops and make for sweeter wine. Harvesting in multiple tries is actually mandatory for both appellations, as it allows the fruit to develop a healthy and pure flavor, or it results in grapes getting eaten by botrytis. Although neither label mimics the honeylike unctuousness of Sauternes wines, they offer flavorful wines that pair well with a great array of foods.

Other remarkable AOPs within Côteaux-du-Layon include Bonnezeaux AOP and Quarts de Chaume AOP, which offer excellent sweet wines, some made from botrytis-affected grapes. The Grand Cru Quarts de Chaume AOP lies on a 40 hectares sandstone and schist hill and, protected from winds, stays humid thanks to morning dew and mists coming from the Layon River. Needless to say, this climate makes a perfect and cozy nest for the noble rot, which requires producers to harvest their crops manually, in several sessions, to get at least one highly valuable batch of fruit.

Quart de Chaume's annual turnout is under 10,000 cases of wine... One can find Quarts de Chaume's sweet wines at Domaine des Baumard as well as at Château Pierre-Brise, two greatly esteemed producers of Savennières. A good address for the larger-but-rarer Bonnezeaux AOP is Château de Fesles.

Seven other villages are qualified to append their names to Côteaux-du-Layon AOP: Beaulieu-sur-layon, Chaume, Faye d'Anjou, Rablay-sur-Layon, Rochefort-sur-Loire, Saint-Aubin-de-Luigne and Saint-Lambert-du-Lattay. Their wines must reach higher minimum must weights and are harvested at lower maximum yields. Chaume's wines, with a minimum of 80 grams of residual sugar per liter, display an exceptional depth, but have been labeled under the Côte-du-Layon appellation since 2009, when producers of rival Quarts du Chaume scuttled the simple Chaume Premier Cru designation. Once Quarts du Chaume gained Grand Cru status in 2011, the INAO re-classified the wines of Chaume as Premier Cru.

Anjou AOP wines, made from Cabernet Franc, are known to be of good value, but the sturdier rouges of the Anjou-Villages AOP often outweigh the simpler designation by reinforcing their Cabernet Franc with some Cabernet Sauvignon. Generally, the Gamay grape are responsible for Anjou's brightest red wines but is often left out of classic Anjou reds.

Château de Goulaine.
This 1,000 year-old Château in the Loire Valley is reputed to be France's and
one of Europe's oldest wine producing estates.

Saumur AOP

As the focal point of Loire's sparkling wine production, Saumur also produces dry white wines, rosés and reds. Altogether, the four types of wine are all covered by the Saumur AOP label, rosé being the newest addition to the list. Prior to 2016, Saumur's rosé wines were bottled as Cabernet de Saumur AOP. Furthermore, Saumur Blanc could be made of Sauvignon Blanc and Chardonnay, but the white wine has a reputation to hold and is now therefore required to be entirely made of Chenin Blanc. Saumur Rouge, on the other hand, still allow a mélange of Cabernet Franc, Cabernet Sauvignon and Pineau d'Aunis. On an important note, over 50% of the grapes grown in Saumur go towards the production of Saumur AOP sparkling wines or to Crémant de Loire AOP and its méthode traditionnelle. The latter is the most promising in terms of taste, as it allows an interesting blend of Touraine and Anjou-Saumur fruit and holds less restrictions regarding grape usage.

Saumur's soft, chalky tuffeau limestone soils offers quality nutrients that grape vines simply love. The limestone actually gets more compact and carries more iron and shale as one gets closer to the town of Champigny, also known as the "field of fire"... About 8 villages bear the means to produce the Saumur-Champigny red wine, often described as a light, elegant and floral interpretation of the Cabernet Franc grape. One of the latest cru to achieve AOP status was Haut-Poitou, in late 2011, as the Vin Délimité de Qualité Supérieure designation was eliminated. Located on the eastern edge of Saumur and about 50 miles south of Chinon, Haut-Poitou grows Sauvignon Blanc and Sauvignon Gris, destined to white wines, and Cabernet Franc, the dominating grape in the area's red and rosé wines.

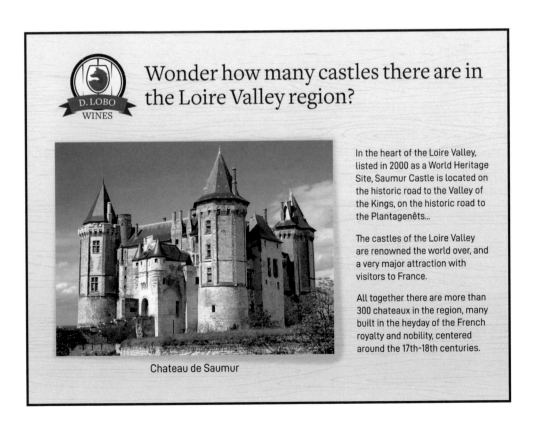

Location and geography

The region of Anjou-Saumur is located to the east of the Pays Nantais.

Climate

Its climate can be described as maritime on the coast and continental when moving inland, and the region experiences humidity.

Soil composition

Blue schist mixed with volcanic debris compose the region's soils.

Grape varieties

White
- Chenin Blanc (locally known as Pineau)

Red
- Cabernet Franc (locally known as Breton)
- Grolleau (devoted to rose wines)
- Gamay
- Pineau d'Aunis
- Cabernet Sauvignon

Some Anjou producers

- **Domaine de Bablut**
- **Domaine des Baumard**
- **Pascal Cailleau**
- **Vincent Ogereau**

Anjou-Saumur appellations

- Anjou AOP
- Chenin Blanc, Cabernet Franc, and Grolleau
• Dry red, white, and rose wines are produced here.

- Anjou-Villages AOP
- Cabernet Franc
• Dry red wines are produced here.

- Saumur AOP
- Chenin Blanc and Cabernet Franc
• Famous for Chenin Blanc sparkling wines.

- Saumur-Champigny AOP
- Cabernet Franc
• Dry red and rose wines are produced here.

- Savennieres AOP
- Chenin Blanc
• Drier styles of Chenin Blanc are produced here.
▶ North of the Loire River. Steep, south-facing hillsides.

- Bonnezeaux AOP
- Chenin Blanc
• Sweet wines are produced here.
▶ South of the Loire River, on the bank of the Layon River.
Humid. Late-harvest, botrytis-affected grapes.

- Quarts-de-Chaume AOP
- Chenin Blanc
• Sweet wines are produced here.
▶ South of the Loire River, on the bank of the Layon River.
Humid. Late-harvest, botrytis-affected grapes.

- Coteaux du Layon AOP
- Chenin Blanc
• Sweet wines are produced here.
▶ South of the Loire River, on the bank of the Layon River.

- Coteaux de l'Aubance AOP
- Chenin Blanc
• Sweet wines are produced here.
▶ South of the Loire River, on the bank of the Layon River.

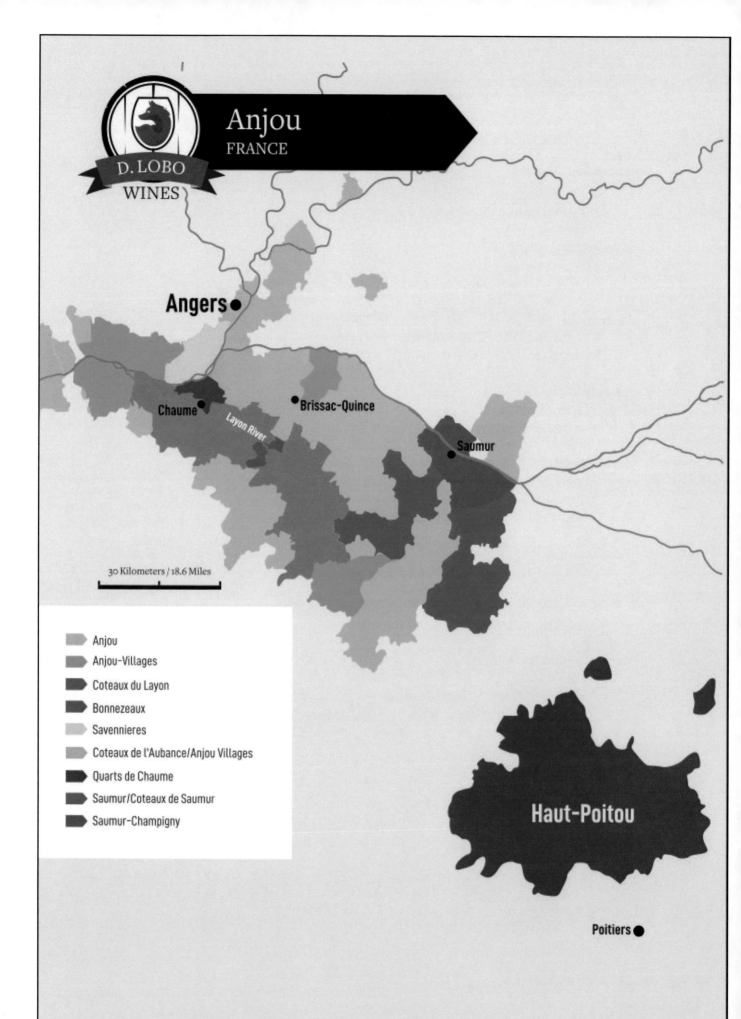

Anjou
FRANCE

D. LOBO
WINES

Angers

Chaume
Layon River
Brissac-Quince
Saumur

30 Kilometers / 18.6 Miles

Anjou
Anjou-Villages
Coteaux du Layon
Bonnezeaux
Savennieres
Coteaux de l'Aubance/Anjou Villages
Quarts de Chaume
Saumur/Coteaux de Saumur
Saumur-Champigny

Haut-Poitou

Poitiers

Touraine

Historically, Touraine and its Bourgueil and Chinon regions are known to host the best and most age-worthy red wine of the Loire. With their raspberry and green tobacco aromas, and their silky acidity, Bourgueil AOP, Saint-Nicolas-de-Bourgueil AOP and Chinon AOP – this one especially - truly set the standard for classic, terroir Loire Cabernet Franc wines (all three appellations require a majority of that grape in their final wines). Chinon soils are made of three types: tuffeau, clay and the sandy varennes. Tuffeau is more commonly found on Chinon's hills, whereas varennes soils are located near the Vienne river, which itself feeds into the Loire.

The south-facing tuffeau soils of Chinon are responsible for the delectable, age-worthy vins de tuffe and provide a small amount of white wine as well, crafted from Chenin Blanc. Contrastingly, Bourgueil, and most particularly Nicolas-de-Bourgueil's more alluvial soils offer red et rosé wines that are much lighter and bright in style.

Up north lie the communes of Montlouis-sur-Loire and Vouvray, on opposite shores of the Loire river. With its tuffeau limestone soil and incredible underground grid of cellar tunnels, Vouvray AOP stands as Touraine's largest white wine producer. Vouvray's sweet whites are mainly juiced from Chenin Blanc but will sometimes – only rarely – contain the more rustic Orbois grape. The levels of sweetness for Vouvray wines vary between sec, sec-tendre (off-dry), demi-sec, moelleux and liquoreux, and are usually based on the quirks and "personality" of each vintage. Bubbly wines – pétillant or Mousseux and crafted by méthode traditionnelle - are also produced in the region and even tend to replace other wines during cooler years. The wines of Montlouis-sur-Loire AOP tend to have a similar style to Vouvray's, as Moutlouis used to be a part of that region. However, the Orbois grape is not allowed in Montlouis-sur-Loire's wines.

While Chenin Blanc has largely been the majority grape in Touraine whites, a 2016 encépagement proceeded to replace the classic style by requiring the region's white wines to contain Sauvignon Blanc and a maximum 20% of Sauvignon Gris. Rouge and rosé varieties, on the other hand, include Gamay – sold locally as primeur -, Grolleau, Pineau d'Aunis and Cabernet Franc grapes, and are not limited to those.

Producing superior pétillant and mousseux wines, the villages of Amboise, Azay-le-Rideau, Chenonceaux, Mesland and Oisly are allowed to append their name to the Touraine AOP designation. The Touraine Noble-Joue AOP, put in effect circa 2011, was created specifically for the Touraine Noble-Joue rosé wines, which recreate a classic style of vin gris made of Gris Meunier (Pinot Meunier), Malvoisie (Pinot Gris) and Pinot Noir..

Other Touraine appellations include Côteaux-du-Loire AOP and the newer Côteaux-du-Vendomois AOP. The first designation covers red blends as well as rosés made from the Pineau d'Aunis grape, and its white wines exclusively contain Chenin Blanc. Jasnières AOP bottles the best Chenin Blanc of Côteaux-du-Loire, often similar to but greener than Vouvray's. Côteaux-du-Vendomois, parallelly, produces wines of all three colors but is especially good with 100% Pineau d'Aunis dry rosés.

On the eastern edge of Touraine, Cheverny AOP crafts bright, Pinot Noir and Gamay-based reds as well as lean whites made mostly from Sauvignon Blanc. Touraine is also home to Cour-Cheverny AOP, which makes dry and off-dry wines out of the local Romorantin grape. Going south, the Valencay AOP bottles Sauvignon Blanc whites as well as Gamay, Pinot Noir and Côt-based red and rosés. Interestingly enough, the French appellation also covers goat milk cheeses!

The Loire Valley hosts over 4,000 wineries that produce an eclectic array of elegant and high-quality wines, such as racy whites, refreshing rosés, reds that favor fruit over force and sumptuous sweet and sparkling wines that even rival the worldly renowned region of Champagne. The Loire Valley is actually second biggest sparkling wine producer after Champagne.

Location and geography

Touraine is located to the east of Anjou-Saumur.

Climate

The climate is continental and has less maritime influence as vineyard locations shift inland toward the east.

Soil composition

The region's soils are mainly composed of tuffeau (soft, limestone), clay and varennes.

Grape varieties

White
- Chenin Blanc
- Sauvignon Blanc
- Orbois
- Pinot Gris
- Romorantin

Red
- Cabernet Franc
- Pinot Noir
- Gamay
- Groslot (Grolleau)
- Pineau d'Aunis
- Cot (Known as Malbec)
- Gris Meunier (Known as Pinot Meunier)

Some Touraine producers

- **Philippe Alliet**
- **Yannick Amirault**
- **Bernard Baudry**
- **Charles Joguet**

Touraine appellations

- Touraine AOP
- Chenin Blanc, Sauvignon Blanc, Sauvignon Gris, red and rosé varieties include, Gamay, Groslot, Pineau d'Aunis, and Cabernet Franc.
• White, red, and rose wines are produced here.
▸ In recognition of their superior wines, five villages are allowed to add their name to the basic appellation:
- Mesland
- Azay-le-Rideau
- Amboise
- Oisly
- Chenonceaux

- Chinon AOP
- Cabernet Franc and small amounts of Chenin Blanc
• Dry red and white wines are produced here.
▸ South bank of the Loire River.

- Bourgueil AOP
- Cabernet Franc and small amounts of rosé wines
• Dry reds, and rosé wines are produced here.
▸ North bank of the Loire River.

- Saint-Nicolas-de-Bourgueil AOP
- Cabernet Franc and small amounts of rosé wines
• Dry reds, and rosé wines are produced here.
▸ North bank of the Loire River.

- Vouvray AOP
- Chenin Blanc and the Orbois grape is allowed but rarely used
• Sparkling, dry, off-dry, and sweet wines (moelleux) are produced here.
▸ North bank of the Loire River.

- Touraine Noble-Joue AOP
- Gris Meunier (Pinot Meunier), Malvoisie (Pinot Gris), and Pinot Noir
- Blend wines of Gris Meunier (Pinot Meunier), Malvoisie (Pinot Gris), and Pinot Noir.
- South bank of the Cher River and north bank of the Inder River.

- Côteaux du Loire AOP
- Pineau d'Aunis and Chenin Blanc
- Red blends and rose wines are produced here.
- North and south bank of the Loir River.

- Jasnières AOP
- Chenin Blanc
- Sparkling, dry, off-dry, and sweet wines (moelleux) are produced here.
- North bank of the Loire River.

- Côteaux de Vendomois AOP
- Pineau d'Aunis
- Dry rose and small amounts of red and white wines are produced here.
- North and south bank of the Loire River.

- Cheverny AOP
- Pinot Noir, Gamay, Romorantin, and Sauvignon Blanc
- Dry and off-dry white and red wines are produced here.
- South bank of the Loire River.

- Cour-Cheverny AOP
- Pinot Noir, Gamay, Romorantin, and Sauvignon Blanc
- Dry and off-dry white and red wines are produced here.
- South bank of the Loire River.

- Valencay AOP
- Pinot Noir, Gamay, Côt and Sauvignon Blanc
- Red, rosé and white wines are produced here.
- North and south bank of the Cher River.

- Montlouis-sur-Loire AOP
- Chenin Blanc
- Sparkling, dry, off-dry, and sweet wines (moelleux) are produced here.
- South bank of the Cher River and north bank of the Inder River.

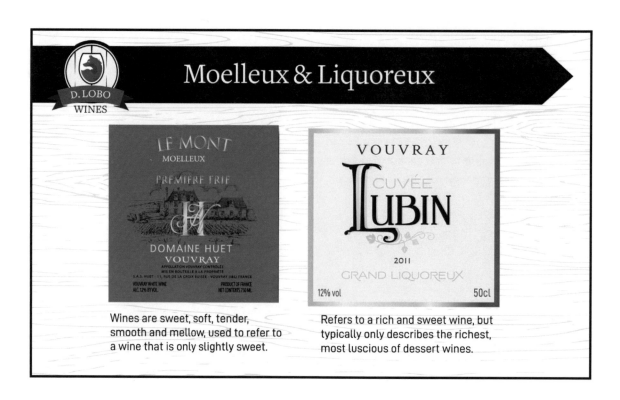

Moelleux & Liquoreux

Wines are sweet, soft, tender, smooth and mellow, used to refer to a wine that is only slightly sweet.

Refers to a rich and sweet wine, but typically only describes the richest, most luscious of dessert wines.

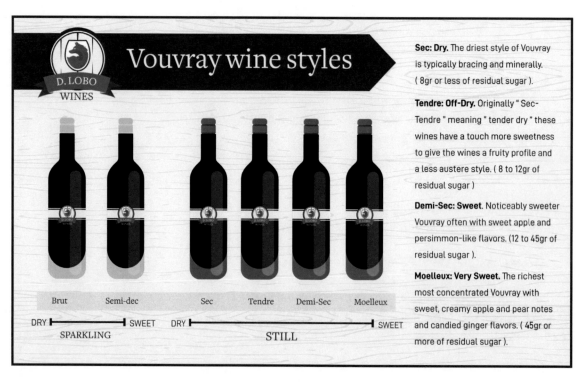

Vouvray wine styles

Sec: Dry. The driest style of Vouvray is typically bracing and minerally. (8gr or less of residual sugar).

Tendre: Off-Dry. Originally " Sec-Tendre " meaning " tender dry " these wines have a touch more sweetness to give the wines a fruity profile and a less austere style. (8 to 12gr of residual sugar)

Demi-Sec: Sweet. Noticeably sweeter Vouvray often with sweet apple and persimmon-like flavors. (12 to 45gr of residual sugar).

Moelleux: Very Sweet. The richest most concentrated Vouvray with sweet, creamy apple and pear notes and candied ginger flavors. (45gr or more of residual sugar).

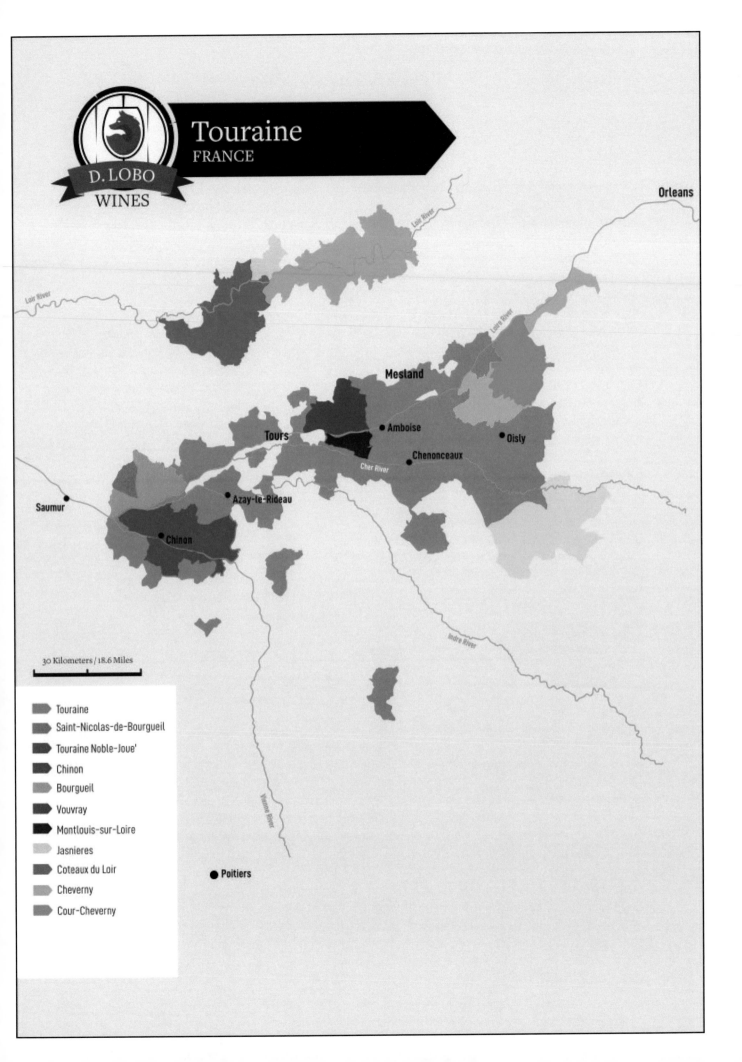

Touraine
FRANCE

D. LOBO WINES

Orleans

Mesland

Tours
• Amboise
• Oisly
• Chenonceaux

• Azay-le-Rideau

Saumur

• Chinon

Poitiers

30 Kilometers / 18.6 Miles

Touraine
Saint-Nicolas-de-Bourgueil
Touraine Noble-Joue'
Chinon
Bourgueil
Vouvray
Montlouis-sur-Loire
Jasnieres
Coteaux du Loir
Cheverny
Cour-Cheverny

Central Vineyards

Located in the heart of France, the Loire's Central Vineyards form a uniform and visually satisfying strip of planted acres, from where the river curves and towards the Atlantic Coast. The area grows the Loire Valley's best Sauvignon Blanc and Pinot Noir, and the continental climate reigning over the region most probably has something to do with it... The cold region's winters may endanger the crops by bringing destructive winds and biting frost, and its short summers do not make the task easy either, but the Central Vineyard wines are truly exceptional during warmer vintages.

The very best expression of Sauvignon Blanc can actually be found in Sancerre AOP as well as in Pouilly-Fumé AOP. Straddling the river, these two appellations are responsible for the classic, youthful, herbaceous and fresh Loire wine style. Other descriptions of the wine tend to paint vibrancy, subtlety and a mastered complexity. Comprising caillotes, silex and terres blanches (white grounds) Sancerre's soils are specially to thank for those delectable drinks. Caillotes, a stony soil, is made of fossils, and Silex, which continues into Pouilly-Fuissé, across the river, is a broad synonym for flint. Terres blanches, on the other hand, is a type of Kimmeridgian clay, almost like the one that tapers Chablis' grounds.

DIDIER DAGUENEAU
The late, passionate Didier Dagueneau famously rebaptized his top Pouilly-Fumé bottling as "Silex". Along others, he did not hesitate to experiment with new oak instead of using the classic stainless steel that is generally used to age Sancerre and Pouilly-Fumé wines. Dagueneau's wines actually resemble Bordeaux whites more than it does traditional Loire Sauvignon Blancs.

While the Pouilly-sur-Loire AOP is reserved for the white wines that are produced from the Chasselas fruit, the Sancerre AOP covers reds and rosés crafted from the Pinot Noir grape. Other Central Vineyards designations include Menetou-Salon AOP, which produces Sancerre like Sauvignon Blanc and Pinot Noir wines, as well as Reuilly AOP, Quincy AOP and Côteaux du Giennois AOP - all three producing various expressions of Sauvignon Blanc. While Reuilly's rouge is purely made of Pinot Noir, its best rosés are juiced from the Pinot Gris grape, making the wine a pale but delicious vin gris. Quincy, on the other hand, only produces white wines, and Côteaux du Giennois is known for red and rosé blends of Pinot Noir and Gamay.

East of Touraine is located Orléans AOP, which was promoted as a Vin Délimité de Qualité Supérieure in 2006. The AOP produces all three colors of wines and mainly uses the Pinot Meunier fruit for its rouge, and Chardonnay for its white. Its sister appellation Orléans-Cléry AOP contrastingly only allows red wines, produced only from the Cabernet Franc grape.

Grape varieties

White
- Sauvignon Blanc
- Chasselas
- Chardonnay
- Pinot Gris

Red
- Pinot Noir
- Cabernet Franc
- Gamay
- Pinot Meunier

Climate

The region's climate is continental.

Soil composition

Silex, terres blanches and caillottes are found in the area's soils.

What is the difference between Sancerre and Pouilly-Fumé?

Pouilly-Fumé tends to be a little broader, softer, slightly less vibrant and aromatic than Sancerre.

Sancerre can have a smoky character, especially those from flint (silex) soils, though this can also be true of Sancerre grown on flint.

Some Central Vineyards producers

- **Gérard Boulay**
- **Henri Bourgeois**
- **Vincent Pinard**
- **Domaine Vacheron**

Central Vineyards appellations

- Sancerre AOP
- Sauvignon Blanc and Pinot Noir
- Dry red and white wines are produced here
▸ Western bank of the Loire River

- Pouilly-Fumé AOP
- Sauvignon Blanc and Pinot Noir
- Dry white wines are produced here
▸ Eastern bank of the Loire River

- Pouilly-sur-Loire AOP
- Chasselas
- Dry white wines are produced here
▸ North bank of the Loire River

- Menetou-Salon AOP
- Sauvignon Blanc and Pinot Noir
- Dry red and white wines are produced here
▸ To the west of Sancerre. Western bank of the Loire River

- Reuilly AOP
- Sauvignon Blanc, Pinot Gris and Pinot Noir
- Dry white, red and rosé wines are produced here
▸ Southwest bank of the Cher River

- Quincy AOP
- Sauvignon Blanc
- Dry white wines are produced here
▸ Southwest bank of the Cher River

- Côteaux du Giennois AOP
- Sauvignon Blanc, Pinot Noir and Gamay
- Dry white wines and red blends are produced here
▸ North bank of the Loire River

- Orléans AOP
- Pinot Meunier and Chardonnay
- Red, white and rosé wines are produced here

- Orléans-Cléry AOP
- Cabernet Franc
- Dry red wines are produced here

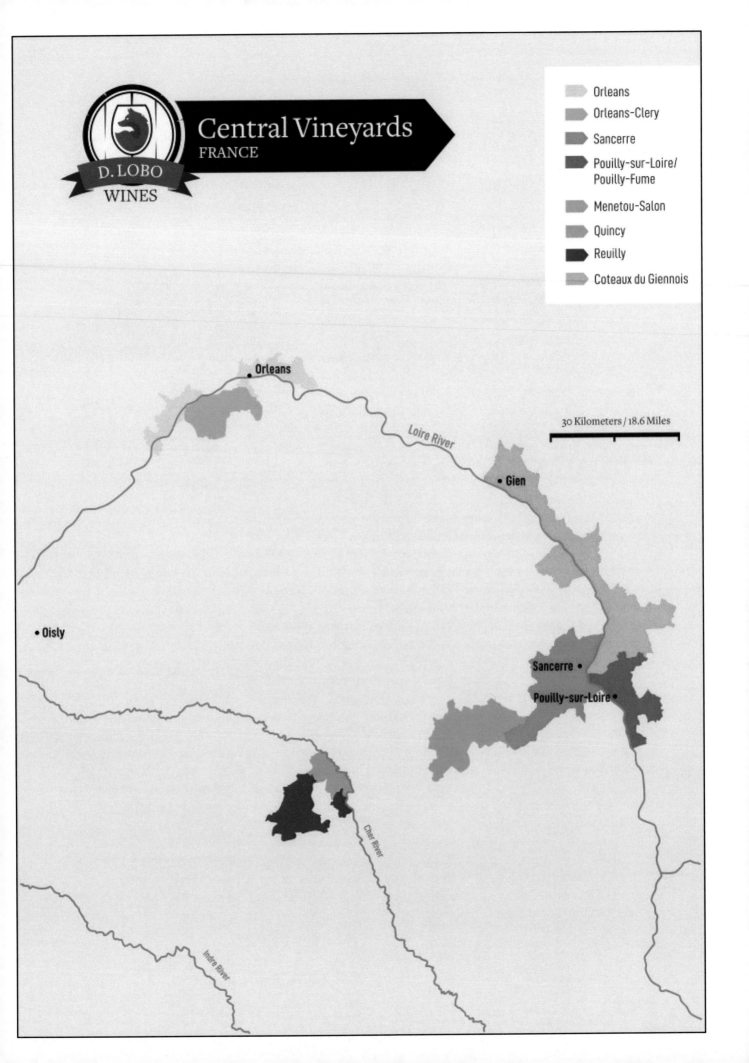

A GLANCE AT ALSACE

Historical Background

Alsace is another one of France's wine regions that will make your curious mind travel through centuries and want to learn more about the country's incredibly rich and deep-rooted history. During the Middle Ages, Alsace actually belonged to the Germanic Holy Roman Empire, and later became the terrain for countless wars driven by political dominance. When France became a centralized state in the 1400 and 1500s, the fresh country upset one of Europe's most powerful dynasties: the Spanish Habsburg family. The religious Thirty Years War then followed between France and the Habsburgs, from 1618 to 1648, and gradually transformed into a full-on European War, opposing French armies to the power-hungry governments. In 1639, France successfully made Alsace a part of its state, but the war only truly ended about a decade later, in 1648, with the Treaty of Westphalia. France will have been left alone by its neighbors for about two centuries before Germany seized Alsace along with Lorraine in 1871, end of the Franco-Prussian War. The Alsace-Lorraine territory became independent for a very short period of time after German Emperor Wilhelm stepped down, marking the end of World War. Within a month, however, French armies proudly reclaimed the region and its capital city, Strasbourg. Alsace will then remain French despite the Nazi shortly occupying the territory in the early 1940s. As of 2016, Alsace, Lorraine and the region of Champagne were grouped under one title: the Grand Est region. A decision that largely displeased the Alsace inhabitants, who did not want to see their culturally rich region merged with two historically divergent ones...

Evidence of winegrowing in the region of Alsace first points to the first millennium. About 160 villages had already been planting and cultivating grapevines by the year 1000, but the trend truly picked up in the 16th century, right before being brought to down to ashes by the violent Thirty Years War... The vineyards of Alsace were only brought back to life after World war I, and a lot of the region's current crops therefore date back to 1945 and later. As German wines maintained their sweetness, Alsatian wines became more dry, intense and pair better with food. Alsace was the last major French winemaking area to reach AOC status in 1962.

Divided into the Haut-Rhin and Bas-Rhin departments, Alsace also happens to be isolated by the rest of France behind the Vosges Mountains, in the west of the country. These mountains are responsible for the "shadow effect", which make Alsace one of France's driest and sunniest, semi-continental climates.

As a result of this exceptional weather, more than two-thirds of the region's Grand Cru vineyards come from the Haut-Rhin. Alsatian vineyards form a belt all the way along the foothills of the Vosges. The best crops enjoy plenty of southeastern sunlight and allow the area's fruit to ripen with an impressive regularity. The region's vines also benefit from an extremely fertile and varied mix of soils comprising chalk, clay, granite, gravel, grés de Vosges (a pink sandstone specific to Alsace) limestone, loess, schist and other volcanic sediment.

A lot of Alsatian villages thus have significantly different soil structures, making the region an eclectic source of grape varieties. While granite and schist can be found in the steeper parts of the Vosges, its lower slopes are composed of limestone and its foothills sit on fertile alluvial clay and gravel.

Overall, Alsace represents 20% of France's total AOP white wine production. In fact, 90% of the region's AOP wine is white, making white grapes such as Gewurztraminer, Muscat, Pinot Gris and Riesling – also known as the noble grapes - the most cultivated in the area. These four varieties can be found in premier cru vineyards and are nearly the only fruit present on Alsatian grand cru sites. Also known as the Vin d'Alsace AOP, the Alsace AOP appellation covers the noble grapes but also the regional Chasselas fruit (Gutedel), Pinot Blanc (Klevner), Pinot Noir and Sylvaner. It is important to know that all varietally labeled Alsace AOP bottles must contain 100% of the grape indicated on the label, for the exception of Pinot Blanc, which is often paired in bottles with the similar Auxerrois fruit. The latter can, interestingly, be labeled as Pinot Blanc. If no grape is listed on a bottle's label, then the wine is a blend. Together, Pinot Blanc and Auxerrois make up the largest volume of the Alsace AOP turnout. Additionally, any white wine labeled simply as Pinot can be made of any Pinot variety, such as Auxerrois, Blanc, Gris and Noir.

Dry, intense and alcoholically stronger than its German sister, the Riesling grape is Alsace's most planted fruit and is often the last of the noble four to ripen. Their acidity and minerality make some of the planet's driest and most age-worthy white wines. On the other hand, the spicy and smoky Pinot Gris wine, formerly known as the Tokay d'Alsace, is Alsace's best expression of the namesake fruit. As for Muscat, the grape makes perfectly fragrant and floral wines, and is about as aromatic and lowly acidic as the stronger and Gewurztraminer grape, which displays more sweet, spicy and tropical notes and makes for drier but liqueur-like wines.

The Gewurztraminer grape is a pink variant of the traditional Traminer, and replaced the original fruit in the region's planted acres in the 1800s. A similarly pink but less fragrant clone of the Traminer, the Klevener grape, can be found in the commune of Heiligenstein in the Bas-Rhin department and is used to craft the acidic Savagnin rosé, or Klevener de Heiligenstein. The eponym commune as well as the towns of Bourgheim, Gertwiller, Goxwiller and Obernai all bottle their own variation of the high-end Savagnin rosé under the Alsace AOP designation.

Contrastingly, Alsace also makes cheaper wines, often blended, that are ironically known as "noble mixtures", or "Edelzwicker". Any Alsace AOP wine labeled with this term does not need to be vintage-dated and can contain either one, or several grapes. No grape percentage needs to be indicated on the bottle either.

Some of Alsatian producers proudly present their blends as the best terroir option for quality, superior wines. These passionate winemakers, like Marcel Deiss, tend to vinify their grapes together and craft their wine under one vineyard name. Another designation, the unofficial "gentil" term, was actually created to label blends containing a minimum of 50% noble grapes – any other Alsace AOP grape may be used to complete the blend but must be aged separately.

In 1975 appeared a new Alsatian appellation: the Alsace Grand Cru AOP. The Schlossberg vineyard was the only site that benefited from the designation until 49 additional vineyards joined in two waves, one in 1983 and the other in 1992. The Kaefferkopf Grand Cru was the last one to make the list, circa 2007. It was only in 2011, however, that each vineyard received its very own appellation, loosening restrictions regarding grape varieties and wine techniques required for each Alsace Grand Cru. The Alsace Grand Cru AOP wines solely contain noble grapes from the region, and hand-harvesting is mandatory for all of them. Bottles are generally single-variety, as it used to be required by Wine Law. Grand Cru wines' minimum sugar levels tend to be higher than the Alsace AOPs, and the minimum potential alcohol lies between 11% (Muscat and Riesling) and 12.5% (Gewurztraminer and Pinot Gris) – certain vineyards, however, are required to produce higher levels of alcohol.

With the fast and wide development of the Alsatian Grand Cru system – 51 grands crus measuring up to 80 hectares -, some of the region's producers actually avoid labeling their wines as Grand Cru, as the large amount of vineyards designated as such seems to decrease the label's value, and no intermediary premier cru level has been put in effect. For instance, the Maison Trimbach, which released its 2009 Geisberg wine as Grand Cru, has been selling its Riesling Clos-Sainte-Hune under the simple Alsace AOP designation, even though it contains grapes from the Rosacker grand cru.

In 1984, two designations were inaugurated specifically for sweet, late-harvest wines: Vendanges Tardives (VT) and Sélection de Grains Nobles (SGN). These labels can appear on both Alsace AOP and Alsace Grand Cru AOP wines provided the bottles are made of one, noble grape variety, as well as pass a blind taste test. While the VT favor grape variety purity and the harvest from vines that are in a state of passerillage (overripening), SGN disregards that aspect to instead emphasize the culture of botrytis. Nonetheless, VT and SGN wines are not legally required to be sweet – if SGN bottles tend to be served as dessert, VT wines can be pretty dry. VT is, however, required to show a minimum of 244 grams/liter of sugar for its Muscat and Riesling bottles, and 270 grams/liter for its Gewurztraminer and Pinot Gris. Raising the bar, SGN's sugar levels need to be 276 grams/liter or more and 306 grams/liter or more for the same wines. It is safe to say that Séléction de Grains Nobles Gewurztraminer and Pinot Gris wines are some of the sweetest French wines.

The only red grapes covered by the Alsace AOP designation is the Pinot Noir. It is mainly used for light rouge and rosé wines that can reach higher intensity and depth during warmer vintages. And although Pinot Blanc is the main fruit used for the highly-esteemed sparkling Crémant d'Alsace, it's Noir sister can also be used for the blend. In fact, the Crémant d'Alsace AOP rosé only contains Pinot Noir. Its color comes from maceration or from the saignée method. The fancy appellation also allows Auxerrois, Pinot Gris and Riesling grapes, and is the only designation of Alsace to permit the use of Chardonnay.

Lastly, some famous Alsace wines actually come from its neighboring region, named Lorraine. The area is home to the Côtes de Toul AOP, which produces Pinot Noir reds, Aubin/Auxerrois whites, and rosés mainly made from both Pinot Noir and Gamay. Lorraine is also responsible for the smaller Moselle AOP – named after the Moselle river - where wines of the three colors of crafted mostly from Auxerrois and Pinot Noir vines. Flowing through eastern France and forming the border between Luxembourg and Germany, the eponym stream also finds its way through the Mosel valley: one of "Deutschland's" greatest Riesling growing areas.

Location and geography

Alsace is located in the northeastern corner of France along the border with Germany. It lies between the Vosges Mountains to the west and the Rhine River to the east. The Vosges Mountains create a rain shadow protecting the region from the harsh, rainy weather coming from Northern France and the Atlantic.

The region is divided in half along the departmental boundaries of:

- **Bas-Rhin**, in the north, and has lower elevation and less protection from the Vosges.
- **Haut-Rhin**, in the south, has higher elevation, the best vineyards are located here.

Climate

Cool continental, because of the northerly latitude. Dry sunny summers due to the rain shadow of the Vosges Mountains. Alsace is one of the driest regions in France.

Topography and aspect

Vineyards are planted on the rolling foothills of the Vosges Mountains. The region also features flat plains along the Rhine River.

Soil composition

There is tremendous diversity across the region because of ancient geologic activity, with various soil types including marl, limestone, gneiss, schist, granite, clay, and volcanic soils.

Grape varieties

White

- Riesling
- Gewurztraminer
- Muscat
- Pinot Gris
- Pinot Blanc
- Sylvaner

Red

- Pinot Noir

Over 90% of Alsace wines are made from white grape varieties. Wines that are labeled by variety must be made entirely from the grape indicated.

Some Alsace producers

- **Léon Beyer**
- **Trimbach**
- **Hugel**
- **Weinbach**
- **Deiss**
- **Gustave Laurentz**
- **Schlumberger**

QUICK FACTS

Viticulture

Long, cool, dry growing season due to the rain shadow cast by the Vosges Mountains. The better vineyards are planted on the lower slopes facing east-southeast.

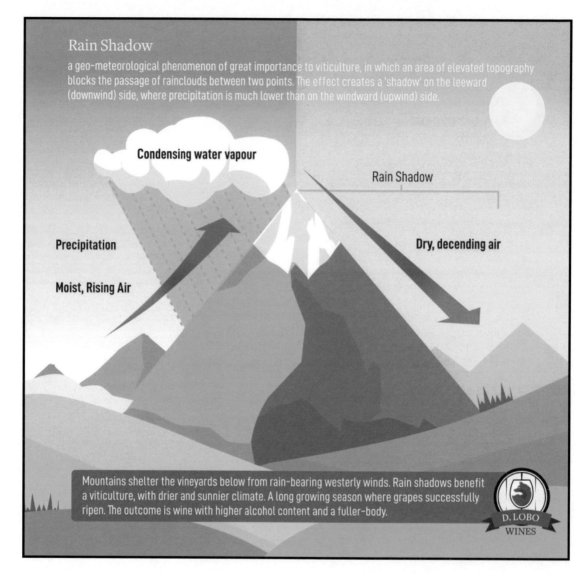

Vinification

Neutral casks are often used for fermentation and aging, and little to no oak is exploited.

Regional Wine Law

Most wines are labeled by reference to the single grape variety utilized.

Alsace appellations

- Alsace/Vin d'Alsace
- One AOP covering the entire region. All Alsace AOP wines must be bottled in the traditional tall, slender bottle called, flûte d'Alsace-style.

Alsace Grand Cru AOP

51 Grand Cru vineyards.
Four grape varieties are allowed to be planted in these vineyards. These varieties are matched with the specific soul type and terroir of the specific vineyard site.

- Riesling
- Gewurztraminer
- Muscat
- Pinot Gris

Crément d'Alsace AOP

Méthode Traditionnelle sparkling wines that are usually made from a blend of grapes. Although Pinot Blanc is the dominant grape for these wines, Chardonnay, Riesling, Pinot Gris and Auxerrois are also permitted in the blend for Crémant d'Alsace.

Rosé wines are solely made from Pinot Noir grapes.

Late harvested wines

Vendange Tardive (VT)
VT stands for late-harvest. Late harvested wines may be affected by botrytis and are full-bodied, but are not always sweet.
Séléction de Grains Nobles (SGN)
Produced in small quantities, SGN wines are always stimulated by botrytis and made only in vintages when growing conditions are met.

Alsace
FRANCE

D. LOBO
WINES

Vosges Mountains

A4

France

Vosges Mountains

Wangen Marlenheim
Wolxheim Strasbourg

A4

Heiligenstein
Barr
Andlau Mittelbergheim

Dambach-la-Ville

Saint-Hippolyte
Ribeauville Bergheim
Hunawihr
Riquewithr
Bennwihr
Kaysersberg
Turckheim
Wintzenheim Colmar
Wettolsheim
Equisheim

Germany

Rouffach
Orschwihr
Guebwiller

20 Kilometers / 12.4 Miles

Berrwiller
Thann

Bas Rhin

Haut Rhin

Alsace AOC

A35

A GLANCE AT JURA

Geographic and viticultural background

Directly neighboring Switzerland, the Jura department is located just south of Alsace and to the east of Burgundy. Named after the Jurassic Era, the beautifully timbered Jura mountains make up for most of the region, but nonetheless benefit from a continental climate and provide fertile terrain for quality vine growth. The mountains' lower hills are made of limestone, marl and also clay – a perfect mix of soils that allows the region to produce wines of all three colors.

Côtes-du-Jura AOP is known to be the standard Jura appellation and allows a great array of red and white grapes. The area's rouges are principally made of Pinot Noir, Poulsard and Trousseau, while its dry whites are generally composed of 100% Chardonnay. The plump Traminer and the Savagnin (or Nature) grape can, in some cases, also be paired with Chardonnay - it is important to note, however, that the Jura's white wines must contain at least 80% of Chardonnay or of Savagnin. As for the lucky rosés, which are usually made in the style of classic vin gris, they can be crafted from all five grapes listed above.The Côtes-du-Jura label also covers the local "vin jaune" (yellow wine) and golden "vin de paille" (straw wine), respectively juiced from Savagnin and Pinot Noir grapes.

Three communal designations saw the light of day in Jura: Arbois AOP, Château Chalon AOP and L'Étoile AOP. The first, home of the scientisits and vaccination pioneer Louis Pasteur, stands as the region's leading wine commune, is used in 12 other towns and crafts all styles of Jura wines. The second, Château Chalon AOP, is actually a commune and not a producer. It is mostly known for its Savagnin vin jaune, an impressively age-worthy wine that is purposely ran through a thorough oxidation process: the grape is left to mature in its topped off cask for 6 years after the harvest – yes, 6 years! -, allowing a yeasty voile (veil) to cover its juice and bring a nutty and spicy aroma to it. Château Chalon's dry yellow wines, for instance, display a delicate and curried flavor that makes them truly original and outstanding. The region's vins jaunes are also required to be bottled in the emblematic 62-centiliter "clavelin", a square-ish shaped bottle that has been used specifically for these wines since the 18th century. Contrastingly, poor vintages can result in their declassification, only allowing them to be labeled as the more generic Côtes-du-Jura AOP.

The white-wine-only Étoile AOP label allows Chardonnay, Poulsard and Savagnin grapes, usually bottled after being oxidized like Château Chalon's jaune. Fun fact: the AOP (a direct translation of "star") was named after a local fossil that itself takes the shape of a pentagram.

Not so fun fact: Jura requires very specific levels oxidation for its white wines, which therefore leads different styles of whites to all standardize more strictly than others. Grape varieties are not even featured on their labels and makes it confusing for consumers

The region's liquoreux vin de paille, a rarer and thus much appreciated style of wine, can be labeled as Arbois, Côtes-du-Jura or L'Étoile AOP. This sweet and intensely aromatic wine is produced from fully ripe grapes that were traditionally left to dry and shrivel on straw mats for at least 6 weeks following their harvest. While the drying time-frame requirement is still in effect, grapes are now often hung to dry or boxed.

Grapes used for vin de paille are required to weigh more than 320 grams/liter after their drying phase. The fruit is then fermented until it produces at least 14% of alcohol before being aged for a minimum of 3 years, including 18 months in wood casks. Once on the market, Jura's straw wines feature a balanced acidity coupled with a luscious sweetness.

The region is known for its Méthode Traditionnelle Crémant du Jura AOP sparkling wines, which are composed of at least 70% Chardonnay, Pinot Noir and/or Trousseau. Escaping from the same standards, the appellation's rosés are only obligated to contain a minimum of 50% black or gray grape varieties.

Jura is also home to the delicious Macvin du Jura AOP red, white and rosé vins de liqueur. Producers add aged marc to unfermented, fresh grape juice in order to obtain the sweet must. The juice is then left to age in oak barrels for at least 10 months after mutage.

Location and geography

Jura is located south of Alsace and to the east of Switzerland.

Climate

The climate is cool continental, with a harsh cold in the wintertime.

Soil composition

Geologic limestone formations with marl and clay pave the region's grounds.

Topography and aspect

The region's vineyards, found on the mountain's lower slopes, rest upon Jurassic limestone and marl with a substantial amount of clay at the lowest sites.

Grape varieties

White
- Chardonnay
-Savagnin (locally known as Nature, elsewhere Traminer)

Red
- Poulsard (Poulssard)
- Trousseau
- Pinot Noir

Some Jura producers

- **Domaine Berthet-Bondet**
- **Domaine Gavenat**
- **Château-Calon**
- **Champ Divin**

Jura appellations

- **Côtes de Jura AOP**
- **Arbois AOP**
- **L'Étoile**
- **Château Chalon AOP**
- **Crémant du Jura AOP**
- **Macvin du Jura AOP**

Vinification

Vin Jaune

Originating from Château-Chalon, the unique, deep yellow tinted Vin Jaune is solely produced from the Savagnin grape. It is produced in its birthplace but also in Arbois, Côtes du Jura and L'Étoile. Vin jaune stays in oak casks for 6 years to mature and gain its special nutty taste. It is then sold in a clavelin, a 62cl bottle closed with wax, specific to this type of wine. This exceptional wine may be kept for up to 50 years and more. For ideal consumption though, it is recommended to open a Vin Jaune bottle half a day before pouring and drinking, and tasted especially delicious when paired with a local Coq au Vin or trout fish, and when served with comté cheese, nuts, foie gras and dried fruits.

Vin de Paille

Also known as Straw Wine, Vin de Paille is a rare and expensive full-bodied dessert wine that displays a beautifully deep golden or amber color. It is only made in small quantities as the Chardonnat, Poulsard and Savagnin grapes that compose it are all laboriously harvested by hand, selected individually at the very beginning of the picking season. Those grapes, once dried on strawbeds, are then left on racks or suspended in a ventilated place for at least 2 months, where they reach 80% dehydration.

18 liters of must is then obtained from pressing about 100 kg (220 lbs) of grapes. It then ferments slowly before ageing in oak casks for 2 to 3 years, and reaches between 15% and 17% alcohol content.

Vin de Paille is partly known for its medicinal benefits. It is best served chilled as an aperitif, dessert or with foie gras. It can be kept for 50 years.

Macvin du Jura

Best consumed as a dessert or aperitif wine, the amber colored "Macvin" is made from grape juice blended with Franche-Comté "Eau de Vie" liquor, allowing some bottles to reach up to 22% alcohol content. Its maturation process takes at least 12 months in oak barrels. It is best served chilled as an aperitif and is perfect with melon. It can be kept for 25 years.

Rosé and red wines

Jura's red wines owe their excellence to the 3 following prestigious grape varieties Poulsard for finish and fruit, Trousseau for body and tannin and Pinot Noir for color and smoothness. These well-structured, light-colored and fruity wines are aged from 1 to 3 years in oak barrels.

The region's rosé wines are produced by red-wine vinification of the Poulsard grape, strictly from the Jura wine region. The "Onion peel" colored rosé of Arbois and Pupillin display fruity flavors and are best served slightly chilled, and best consumed throughout a meal.

Keeping well for 20 to 30 years, a Trousseau at room temperature, pairs perfectly with meats and cheese. On the other hand, a Poulsard at room temperature is excellent when coupled with appetizers or with regional Charcuterie. It can be kept for ten years.

White wines

The white Jura wines are produced from two grapes, Chardonnay and Savagnin, which are vinified alone or combined. Flowery and fruity wines are produced from the Chardonnay grape, which is the main variety used for the white wines in Jura. The Savagnin, however, is considered the King of the region's grape varieties.

Jura's white wines vary from pale yellow to straw colors, and acquire the special Jura bouquet during their aging in oak casks, in which they mature for up to 4 years.

Served at room temperature, they pair well with entrees, fish and regional dishes cooked in cream and cheese sauce.

Crémant du Jura

The Jura wine region was awarded the appellation Crémant du Jura in 1995. This sparkling wine is produced from Chardonnay, Poulsard, and Pinot Noir grapes and falls under the same strict rules as Champagne. Crémant du Jura comes in Brut or Demi-Sec, white or rosé, from L'Étoile, Arbois or Côtes du Jura.

It is best served chilled as an aperitif, plain or with blackcurrant syrup, with dessert or throughout a meal. It is ready to drink on its release or can be kept a maximum of 10 years.

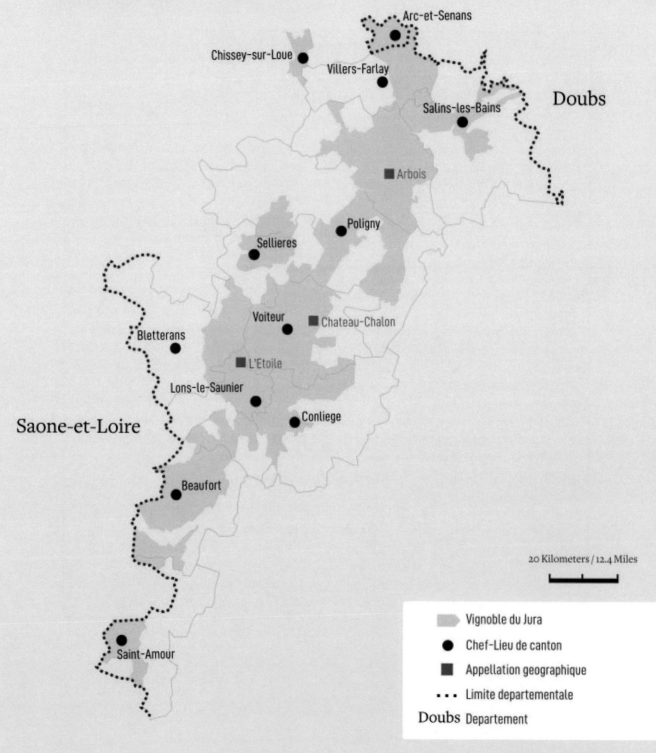

Jura
FRANCE

D. LOBO
WINES

Arc-et-Senans

Chissey-sur-Loue

Villers-Farlay

Salins-les-Bains

Doubs

Arbois

Poligny

Sellieres

Voiteur

Chateau-Chalon

Bletterans

L'Etoile

Lons-le-Saunier

Conliege

Saone-et-Loire

Beaufort

Saint-Amour

20 Kilometers / 12.4 Miles

Vignoble du Jura

Chef-Lieu de canton

Appellation geographique

Limite departementale

Doubs Departement

A GLANCE AT SAVOIE

Geographic and viticultural background

Past the southern border of Jura starts the department of Savoie, home of the northern Alps and premium ski destination. The area owes its continental climate to Lakes Bourget and Léman, which are both surrounded by lush but dispersed vineyards.

The region's main appellation is Vin de Savoie AOP and the majority of its planted acres mainly grow white grapevines, most particularly the Altesse, Chardonnay and Roussanne

fruit, as well as the dominant but lower-quality Jacquere. Of course, Savoie also produces red and rosés, which are mainly made from Gamay, Mondeuse and Pinot Noir. The region is known for its sparkling wines as well, particularly its Vin de Savoie Mousseux and pétillants.

Overall, Vin de Savoie AOP is used by a lot of villages in the region, which simply tend to append their names to the appellation, and in some cases opt for a more local designation. Savoie also hosts a second regional appellation: Roussette de Savoie AOP. Also known as Altesse, the Roussette grape must comprise 100% of the wines produced under the namesake appellation. The Chignin-Bergeron wine, for instance, is entirely made of Roussanne, as Chardonnay cannot be used as a blending grape anymore. The Roussette de Savoie AOP is used by four communes in total: Frangy, Marestel, Monterminod and Monthoux.

A third appellation, Seyssel AOP, covers some of Savoie's best dry, off-dry and Mousseux wines. Located right above Lake Bourget, Seyssel vineyards grow Altesse, Molette and Chasselas, although Altesse usually is the only grape used for Seyssel wines. The area's sparkling wines, however, allow blends of different varieties and only need 10% of the three grapes listed above. To the west of Lake Bourget, Bugey AOP – which covers the communes of Montagnieu and Virieu-le-Grand – is also partly known for its sparkling wines, and especially its bubbly méthode ancestrale rosés (generally known as Bugey-Cerdon). Just like Roussette de Savoie wines, Roussette de Bugey AOP's are 100% made from the Altesse variety.

Lastly, we cannot write about Savoie without mentioning its well-esteemed Crémant wines. Established in 2015, the Crémant de Savoie AOP covers wines mostly made from Jacquere, Altesse and Chardonnay, and allow red varieties as well.

Location and geography

The region of Savoie lies southeast of the Jura departement.

Climate

The climate is continental and moderated by large bodies of water: Lake Bourget and Lake Geneva.

Soil composition

The region's soils are composed of moraines (glacial deposits), alluvial soils, river terraces and rich limestone.

Grape varieties

White
- Jacquère
- Altesse
- Roussanne
- Chasselas
- Gringet

Other white grape varieties

- Mondeuse Blanche, Chardonnay, Aligote, Molette, Marsanne, Pinot Gris, Fruhroter Veltliner, and Verdesse.

Red
- Mondeuse
- Persan

Other red grape varieties

- Gamay, Pinot Noir, Douce Noire, Cabernet Franc, Cabernet Sauvignon, Merlot, Joubertin, and Poulsard.

Savoie appellations

- Vin de Savoie AOP
- Roussette de Savoie AOP
- Seysell AOP
- Bugey AOP
- Bugey Cerdon
- Crémant de Savoie AOP

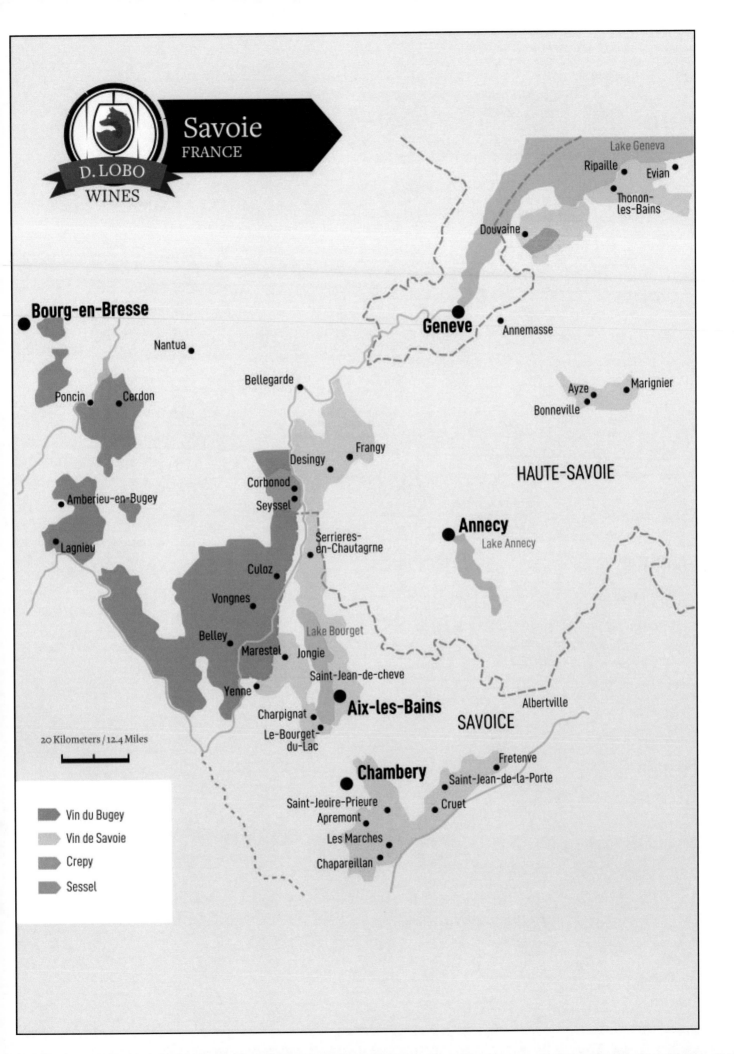

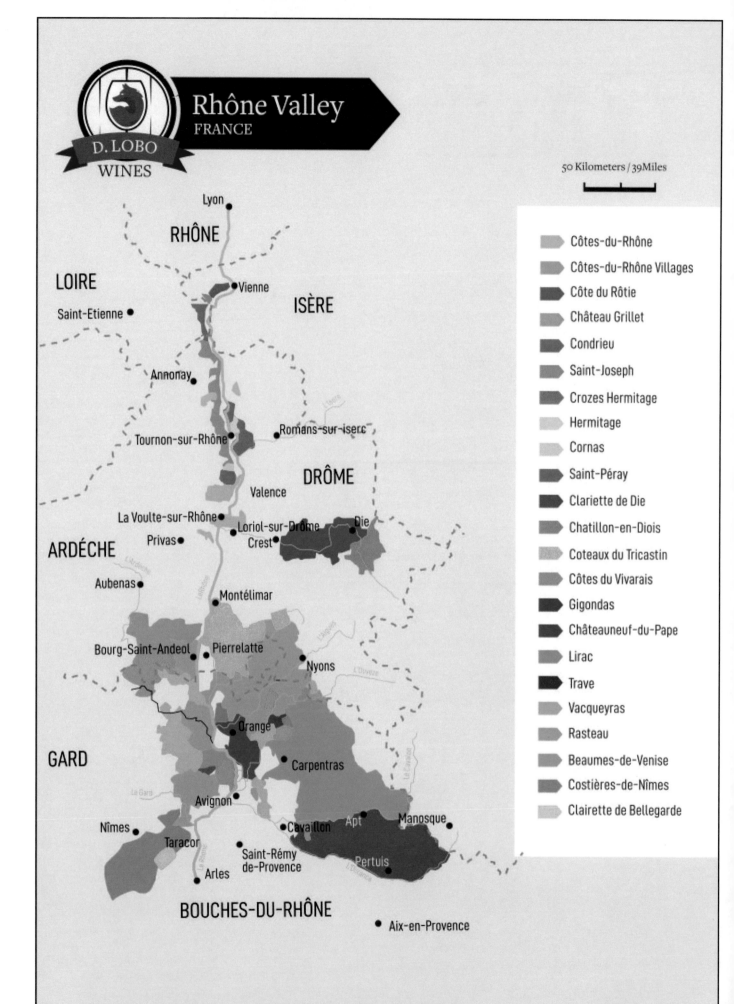

A GLANCE AT THE RHÔNE VALLEY

Historical background

Flowing from Switzerland to the Mediterranean Sea, the Rhône river gives its name to the famous wine growing valley. The Northern Rhône (also known as Rhône-Septentrional) lies just south of Beaujolais and forms a thin ribbon of vineyards funneling from Vienne to Valence. The Southern Rhône (also known as Rhône-Méridional), which bears a different climate and therefore distinct patterns of winemaking than its northern counterpart, runs from the city of Montélimar to the Mediterranean basin.

While the Greeks are actually to thank for the birth of viticulture in France, the Romans were the first to introduce enology in the Rhône Valley, and most particularly in the Southern Rhône, circa 125 BCE. When Greek settlers set foot in Gaul around 600 BCE, the Rhône river served as their main wine trading route, as 10 million liters of wine flowed from Massalia (now Marseilles) to the center of the country. Roman merchants then took over the trade a few centuries later, steadily planting vines in the meridional until appropriating Northern Rhône's grounds around the 1st century. As a wine enthusiast, you have probably heard of the scenic terraces of Vienne, formerly known as the Roman capital, where was elaborated the Syrah vinum picatum, or pitched wine.

Although wine trade took a hit during the aptly named Dark Ages, the Catholic church and its wine-loving monks brought it back to like in the 800th, just like they did in Burgundy. Southern Rhône actually became Pope Clément V's home and therefore turned into the heart of Christian Europe. Châteauneuf-du-Pape and its vineyards however, was not a creation of Clément V but rather of its successor, Pope John XXII. The Domaine stayed in the hands of the papacy until 1791 - its wines were labeled as Vins d'Avignon until the 1800s, before taking on the Châteauneuf appellation. As the Rhône-Méridional's vineyards were the first in France to suffer from the devastating effects of phylloxera, in 1863, many attempts of fraudulent grafting of the region's highest-quality grape varieties were made. To counter this phenomenon, vignerons in Châteauneuf-du-Pape imposed some strict production standards, which were later used as a prototype for the Appellation d'Origine Contrôlée designation system. In 1936, the commune was the very first to achieve AOC status in the country and its wines are among the most esteemed in the world.

Before being brought to English tables in the 18th century, the wines of the Rhône valley made a stop in the Loire basin, helping Rhône bottles make a name for themselves all over France and then abroad. The wines of Hermitage were among the region's best product: described as "manly" for its enveloping intensity, they were appropriated by many négociants in Bordeaux and blended in more generic reds to strengthen their texture and flavor.

Northern Rhône

Northern Rhône has one of the most particular climates in France: enjoying continental weathers, the Septentrional experiences intense temperature changes, rainfall and strong, cold winds. One interesting aspect, however, is that the great Mistral wind, vigorous enough that it could destroy the region's vines, instead makes its trees grow in a southward leaning motion. This specificity allows vines to be protected from the wind but also leaves no opportunity for mildew to consume the crops. The granite and schist-based soils of Northern Rhône also retain heat, helping vineyards survive biting cold episodes. The vineyards of Condrieu, Côte-Rôtie and Hermitage are among those that benefit from these soils, with Condrieu's grounds being rich with powdery mica (arzelle). The rest of Northern Rhône is made of heavier clay soils.

The Syrah grape is emblematic of the Septentrional, and makes the region's wines full-bodied as well as intensely savory. Hints of smokey meat, tart olive and fresh lavender aromas can be tasted in the peppery Syrah wines, which are traditionally fermented in oak barrels by five of the area's appellations: Cornas AOP, Côte-Rôtie AOP, Crozes-Hermitage AOP, Hermitage AOP and Saint-Joseph AOP. Only Cornas bottles wine that is fully made from Syrah, as the other AOPs also allows white grapes in the mix. For instance, Côte-Rôtie ("roasted slope") can add up to 20% Viognier in its blend; the vignerons of Crozes-Hermitage and its simpler named neighbor, Hermitage, are permitted to throw 15% Marsanne and Roussanne in their Syrah concoction; lastly, up to 10% Marsanne and Roussane are fermented with the Syrah variety in the domaines of Saint-Joseph. This "co-fermentation" allows for the wine's ruby color to stabilize all while moderating the levels of tannin.

Syrah wines tend to be stronger and more rustic in the warn vineyards of Cornas – the warmest of Northern Rhône. Luckily protected from the strong Mistral wind, the granite soils of Cornas produce reds that age slowly in the bottle but offer delectable earthy aromas and would make anyone want to sip some of it by a reassuring campfire. As the smallest rouge appellation (only 100 hectares – 247 acres), Cornas is separated in four "lieux-dits", or tiny villages: Les Chaillots, La Côte, Les Mazards and Les Reynards. The most esteemed traditional wines labeled under the AOP are produced by the Auguste Clape domaine, known for fermenting whole clusters of grapes in old half barrels (demi-muids).

The steepest vineyards of France (up to a 55° angle) belong to the Côte-Rôtie appellation which is located in the very north of the Septentrional. The Côte Brun and Côte Blonde, along with the riverside commune of Ampuis, produce the best wines of the "roasted slope" and never fail to be mentioned when talking about the AOP's terroir.

While the Côte Brune offers competitive, intense wines and the Côte Brune produces softer, luscious ones. As for Ampuis, the commune hosts the Côte Rôtie's largest appellation, E. Guigal – which, along with René Rostaing and other producers, is responsible for grand cru standard La Landonne wines. Other quality red wines are yielded in Crozes-Hermitage. Lighter and meant for youthful consumption, they still fiercely compete with the alluring Syrah wines of Hermitage AOP. Facing south, the appellation hosts four highly competent and esteemed producers. The first one is Jean-Louis Chave, and the three others are actually négociants: Delas, Jaboulet and M. Chapoutier. Altogether, they produce the notable Beaume, Les Bessards, Gréffieux, Méal and Péléat wines, but La Chapelle seems to stand out the most. Produced by Jaboulet, the wine was baptized in honor of the Saint-Christophe chapel located atop the hill of Tain-l'Hermitage. The chapel famously hosted heroic knight Henri-Gaspard de Stérimberg, who prolonged his stay after adopting the ascetic lifestyle.

Saint-Joseph, situated opposite the hill of Hermitage and to the north of Cornas, produces a versatile selection of wines that meet rather generic quality levels. The AOP grew larger throughout the years, and now runs through Condrieu AOP, a Viognier white appellation lying right under Côte-Rôtie. Although Condrieu went through a rough patch in the 60s, its rich honey and floral Viognier specialty is now being revived thanks to the efforts of adventurous producers like André Perret and Georges Vernay. The Condrieu monopole Château Grillet AOP also contributes to the resurgence of Viognier wines, but seems to be esteemed for the rarity of production rather than for the wine's taste.

While Cornas and Côte-Rôtie only produce red wines, Crozes-Hermitage, Hermitage and Saint-Joseph also produce some sweet, oily Marsanne and tannic Roussanne-based whites like the ones of Saint-Péray AOP, which only produce these wines, generally in the form of a méthode traditionnelle Mousseux. Hermitage producers like Gérard Chave and Chapoutier usually use either one of the two grapes to craft the scarce, liquoreux vin de paille.

Lastly, we would like to draw your attention on four minor, but notable, appellations located on the Drôme river, affluent of the Rhône: Côteaux de Die AOP, Crémant de Die AOP, Clairette de Die AOP and Châtillon-en-Diois AOP. While Côteaux de Die provides whites made from 100% Clairette, Crémant de Die AOP offers sparkling blancs only partially made of the same grape. On the other hand, Clairette de Die AOP yields two effervescent wine styles known as méthode traditionnelle – which is solely composed of Clairette - and méthode Dioise ancestrale – which interestingly requires a minimum 75% Muscat à Petits Grains. The latter is, as its name suggests, an ancient sparkling wine method that favors bottling without dosage before the product has even done fermenting. Poured into pressurized tanks, méthode ancestrale wines are then rebottled sans liqueur de dosage allowing wines to maintain a demi-sec sweetness, as at least 35 grams/liter of residual sugar remain. Contrastingly, méthode traditionnelle wines only contain a maximum of 15 grams/liter after dosage, giving them a brut style. Lastly, Châtillon-en-Diois AOP provides Gamay-based reds and rosés, as well as Aligoté and Chardonnay based-whites.

Location and geography

The Northern Rhône's vineyards form two narrow ribbons on both sides of the Rhône River. Together, the band of vineyards starts around 15 miles south to Lyon and runs for a good 50 miles from Vienne to Valence.

Climate

The region's climate is continental. The Rhône River, which originates in Switzerland, acts as a climate moderator for the Northern Rhône's vineyards, warming the adjacent slopes and reflecting sunlight up to the vines.

Mistral winds are a prominent airflow that begins in Switzerland near the mouth of the river, picking up speed as it heads south into France and into the Northern Rhône Valley. It slightly warms the area and dries the climate, helping prevent mildew and other molds.

Topography and aspect

The region displays impressive steep hillside vineyards.

Soil composition

Granite and schist are the main components of the region's soils.

Grape varieties

White
- Viognier
- Marsanne
- Roussanne
- Clairette
- Aligoté
- Chardonnay

Red
- Syrah
- Gamay

Some Northern Rhône producers

- **Guigal**
- **Chave**
- **Chapoutier**
- **Saint Cosme**

Viticulture

Vineyards are planted on steep slopes overlooking the river. In the region, vines often have to be staked to the ground in order to stand against the Mistral wind and survive erosion. Roman terraces are still maintained as they make it easier for growers to access their crops.

Vinification

Single-variety wines dominate, with fewer blends than most French regions.

Both white and red wines are usually fermented and aged often in large oak barrels, although many producers choose to ferment their fruit in stainless steel to then age their wines in a combination of new andd ancient oak.

Co-fermentation, used to boost aromatic complexity and lessen tannins in red wines, is also practiced. Some reds are therefore co-fermented with tiny percentages of white grapes to obtain those effects.

Vines located in steep slopes overlooking the Rhône River

Northern Rhône appellations

- **Côte-rôtie AOP**
  - Red wines only, Syrah with a maximum of 20% Viognier
  - ► Ampuis, Côte Brune, and Côte Blonde, heart of the appellation's terroir.

- **Condrieu AOP**
  - White wines only, 100% Viognier

- **Saint-Joseph AOP**
  - Red wines, Syrah with a maximum 10% Roussanne and Marsanne
  - ► White wines, Roussanne and Marsanne

- **Crozes-Hermitage AOP**
  - Red wines, Syrah with a maximum 15% Roussanne and Marsanne
  - ► White wines, Roussanne and Marsanne

- **Hermitage AOP**
  - Red wines, Syrah with a maximum 15% Roussanne and Marsanne
  - ► White wines, Roussanne and Marsanne

- **Cornas AOP**
  - Red wines only, 100% Syrah
  - ► Divided in four quarters (lieux-dits), Les Reynards, La Cote, Les Chaillot, Les Mazards.

- **Saint-Péray AOP**
  - White wines, Roussanne and Marsanne

- **Clairette de Die**
  - Méthode Traditionelle sparkling wines made with Clairette grapes and brut in style.
  - ► Méthode Ancestrale, 75% made with Muscat a Petit Grains grapes and demi-sec in style.

- **Châtillon-en-Diois AOP**
  - Red wines, Gamay
  - ► White wines, Aligoté and Chardonnay

- **Château Grillet AOP**
  - White wines, Viogner

- **Côteaux de Die AOP**
  - White wine, Clairette

- **Crémant de Die AOP**
  - Sparkling wines produced with Clairette grapes

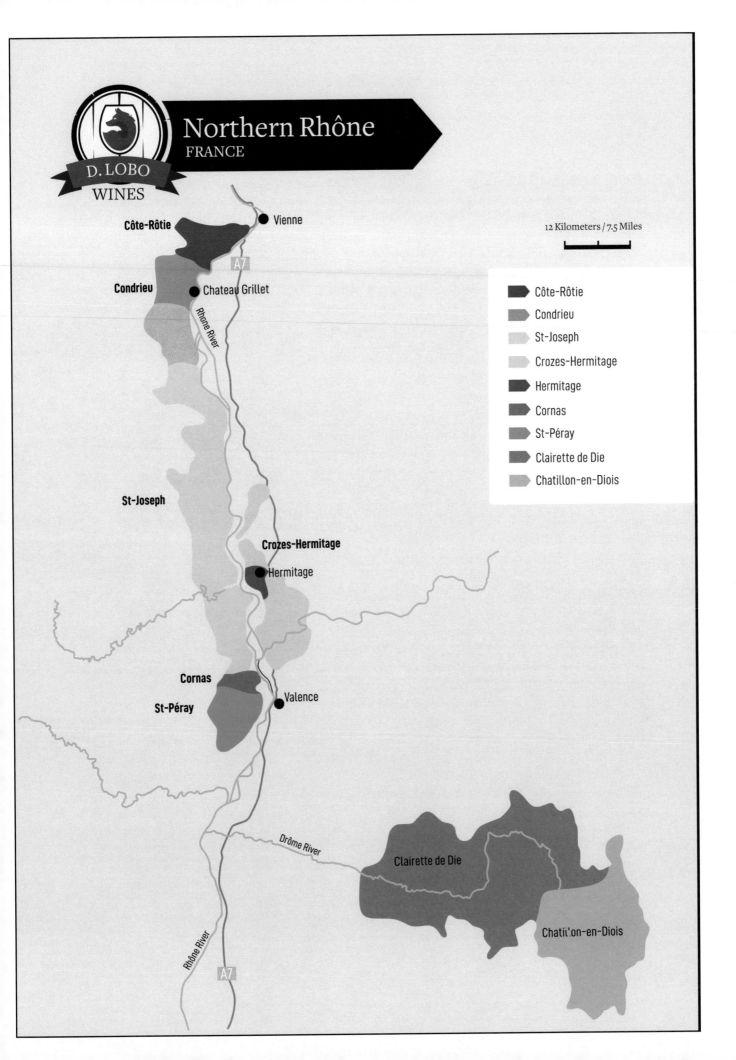

Northern Rhône
FRANCE

D. LOBO
WINES

12 Kilometers / 7.5 Miles

Côte-Rôtie

Vienne

Condrieu
Chateau Grillet

A7

Rhône River

St-Joseph

Crozes-Hermitage

Hermitage

Cornas

St-Péray

Valence

Drôme River

Clairette de Die

Chatii'on-en-Diois

Rhône River

A7

Côte-Rôtie
Condrieu
St-Joseph
Crozes-Hermitage
Hermitage
Cornas
St-Péray
Clairette de Die
Chatillon-en-Diois

Southern Rhône

Unlike its Northern counterpart, the Southern Rhône predominantly produces red wine, and blends in particular. It is also important to note that nearly 95% of the Rhône Valley's winemaking happens in the Méridional and its sand, gravel and clay soils. Enjoying a Mediterranean climate as well, the region's landscape paints low shrubs and dry herbs spread out on a flat windy land. That's right: the unforgiving Mistral does not spare the Southern Rhône either, which leads many of the area's vignerons to plant their vines at a specific angle in order for them to grow upright against the wind. And although the Méridional benefits from lots of sunny days, it also experiences heavy rainfalls.

A few quality grape varieties grow in the region: Carignan, Cinsault, the Spanish Grenache, Mourvèdre and Syrah. All get to flourish on a mix of alluvial soils and post-ice age quartz "galets" – flat, smooth pudding stones. These heat-retaining rocks, which are especially present in Châteauneuf-du-Pape, warm up the vines' roots during colder nights. As the last dominant red variety in the region, Carignan yields fruity wines that, on top of displaying berry notes, also show some surprising hints of bacon... The most planted red grape, Grenache, also makes for sweet berry wines, but are more full-bodied as well as enveloping. And while Cinsault provides a light freshness to Southern Rhône red and rosé wines, Mourvèdre and Syrah bring to the blends a well needed structure as well as a dark ruby color.

If there is one place where blending is done right, it is definitely the illustrious Châteauneuf-du-Pape AOP. As the main appellation in the Méridional, Châteauneuf-du-Pape allows up to 18 different varieties of grapes in its wines while still maintaining high quality standards. Without surprise, the versatile Grenache is the dominant grape in the AOP's wines – Château Rayas, for instance, produces its Châteauneuf-du-Pape red with 100% Grenache. Poles apart, the delectable Château de Beaucastel's rouge comprises Mourvèdre as the main grape and throws every other permitted variety in the blend.

Generally, the Southern Rhône's reds tend to display more ripeness and depth, and often hold stronger alcoholic levels than those of the Septentrional, as the region's producers are required to discard 2% or more of their harvested grapes to lower cases of underripeness. The southern region's wines can actually be the strongest in France: they have to contain a minimum of 12.5% alcohol and can reach up to 15%!

The first Châteauneuf-du-Pape was bottled and sold by the Château La Nerthe estate in 1785, and its authentic papal crest still appears on the bottle's shoulder on all wines that belong to the appellation. Counting 3,000 acres in total, Châteauneuf-du-Pape enjoys an extremely varied soil composition, partly responsible for the plumpness and quality of the AOP's grapes. Producers from the designation also like age their wines in traditional oak barrels to guarantee even stronger essence. Others also experiment thanks to methods like carbonic maceration, barrique aging and different assemblage, and some transfer their barreled wine to bottles as it is sold to create different variations of the same wine.

Châteauneuf-du-Pape

Although Châteauneuf-du-Pape is the highest esteemed appellation in the Méridional, it is neither the largest nor the principal, as these titles go to Côtes du Rhône AOP. In fact, over 60% of the entire Rhône Valley's red (dominant), rosé and white wines are labeled as Côtes du Rhône. The Southern Rhône specifically benefits from its own superior – Grenache, Mourvèdre, and Syrah - red appellation, that 21 communes in the region can append their names to: Côtes du Rhône-Villages AOP.

Five communes, all sharing the same 12.5% minimum alcohol requirement for red wines, reached high enough standards to gain their own appellations. The first, Gigondas AOP, was inaugurated in 1971 for its unique 50% Grenache reds and its rosé wines, yielded from grapes grown on red clay soils. Gigondas wines are very similar to Châteauneuf-du-Pape's and can surely compete with other premium vintages. The next commune to be promoted was Vacqueras AOP (in 1990), whose rustic reds also require to be made from at least 50% Grenache. The label covers a few whites and rosés as well. With similar rouge compositions, Beaumes-de-Venise AOP and Vinsobres AOP respectively made the cut in 2005 and 2006. The dry white and red wine appellation Cairanne AOP was the last to join the emancipated communes, in 2016.

One has to cross the Rhône river to find the red, white and rosé yielding Lirac AOP. Located on the exact opposite of Châteauneuf-du-Pape, the appellation covers four communes that produces wines in the likes of Côtes du Rhône-Villages'. The AOP's vineyards - which are believed to be the first to incubate the phylloxera pest, circa 1863 -, mostly hosts Grenache Noir and Blanc, as well as Bourboulenc and Clairette. Taking a few steps south of Lirac, Tavel AOP awaits dry rosé enthusiast. The appellation is actually the only one in France to only produce rosés (Grenache-based), and is arguably seen as the best.

Further proving Southern Rhône's versatility, the region's Muscat de Beaumes-de-Venise AOP and Rasteau AOP produce fortified vin doux naturel. About 90% of Muscat de Beaumes-de-Venise red, white and rosé wines are produced by a small, local group of winegrowers baptized the Vignerons de Beaumes-de-Venise from grapes that are just as local. Thanks to the mutage process, the appellation's wines comprise pure, natural sugar coming straight from the fruit. As a result, the label's bottles display strong, fresh aromas and a delicious sweetness.

Vins doux naturels of all three colors of wines are also produced under Rasteau AOP in the towns of Cairanne, Rasteau and Sablet, and are actually made from all three colors of Grenache – Noir, Blanc and Gris. Dark to the eye and nutty to the taste, Rasteau red and white wines may respectively be labeled as ambre and tuile, following Rivesaltes' terminology, as they tend to show oxidative traits and are also left to age for three years (or more) before release. The youthful ones, however, are sold under "blanc" for whites and "grenat", for reds. Another designation, "Hors d'âge", is dedicated for wines that have spent at least five years in their sealed tanks. And those that were left to age in open barrels under the harsh rays of the sun – for an even further oxidative style -, are labeled as "rancio".

Côtes du Vivarais, Grignan-les-Adhémar, Lubéron and Ventoux, to name a few, are some other notable AOPs of the Southern Rhône. To the west also lies well-esteemed Costières de Nîmes AOP, which connects the Méridional with Provence and Langueoc (the appellation was actually a Languedoc appellation until 2004 before INAO decided otherwise), and Clairette de Bellegarde AOP. Aside from the latter, which only produces Clairette white wines, each of these appellations produce all three colors of wines mainly from regional grapes, helping protect and showcase the Valley's terroir.

.

Château des Fines Roches

Location and geography

Châteauneuf-du-Pape forms a 30-mile gap between the Northern Rhône and the Southern Rhône..

Climate

The area's climate is mediterranean. The Mistral, along with the Rhône River, help cool the area, and hot summers are moderated by intense diurnal temperatures swings.

Topography and aspect

Flatter plains and broader low, scrubland make can be found towards the Mediterranean Sea.

Soil composition

The region's soils are composed of alluvial clay and other deposits of large river rocks called, galets.

Grape varieties

White
- Roussanne
- Clairette
- Grenache Blanc

Red
- Grenache
- Syrah
- Mourvèdre

90% of the production

The grapes of Châteauneuf-du-Pape

- Grenache (Noir/Blanc/Gris)
- Cinsault
- Counoise
- Picpoul (Noir/Blanc/Gris)
- Terret Noir
- Bourboulenc
- Clairette/Clairette Rose
- Vaccarèse
- Picardan
- Muscardin

Some Southern Rhône producers

- **Domaine de la Janasse**
- **Domaine du Pégaü**
- **Clos des Papes**
- **Rayas**

Viticulture

The region's growers use bush (gobelet) vine training. Many vineyards are planted on flat ground, in the valley.

Vinification

Blends dominate, fewer single-variety wines. Blending of grapes.

Some producers, in some areas, do use oak, although they usually ferment their wines in large oak casks rather than barriques.

No chaptalization is allowed in the region.

Southern Rhône AOC System

- Single Village AOC's
- Côtes du Rhône-Villages (Geographic Designation)
- Côtes du Rhône

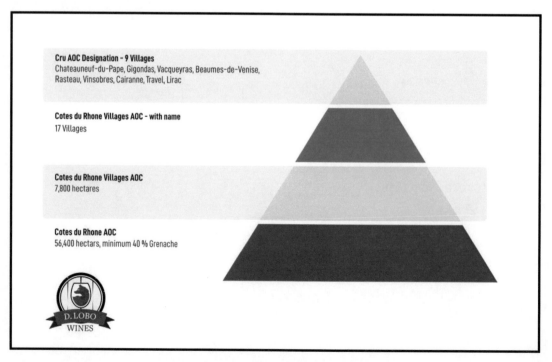

Cru AOC Designation - 9 Villages
Chateauneuf-du-Pape, Gigondas, Vacqueyras, Beaumes-de-Venise, Rasteau, Vinsobres, Cairanne, Travel, Lirac

Cotes du Rhone Villages AOC - with name
17 Villages

Cotes du Rhone Villages AOC
7,800 hectares

Cotes du Rhone AOC
56,400 hectars, minimum 40 % Grenache

Southern Rhône Appellation System Pyramid

VIllage appellations

- Châteauneuf-du-Pape
- • White wines; Blend of local varieties.
- ▸ Red; Grenache-based blends. 14 grape varieties plus variations authorized.

- Gigondas
- • Red wines; Grenache-based blends.

- Vacqueyras
- • White wines; Blend of local varieties.
- ▸ Red and rose wines; Grenache-based blends.

- Tavel
- • Rose wines only. Grenache-based blends.

Other Southern Rhône appellations

- Beaume-de-Venise AOP
- • Red wines; Grenache-based blends.

- Vinsobres AOP
- • Red wines; Grenache-based blends.

- Cairanne AOP
- • White wines; Blend of local varieties.
- ▸ Red wines; Grenache-based blends.

- Lirac AOP
- • White, red, and rose wines; Grenache Noir and Grenache Blanc are prevalent.

- Muscat de Beaumes-de-Venise AOP
- • Vin doux naturel, sweet fortified wines.

- Rasteau AOP
- • Vin doux naturel, sweet fortified wines.
- ▸ Three communes are eligible for the AOP; Rasteau, Cairanne, and Sablet.

- Grignan-les-Adhémar AOP
- •Red wines; Grenache-based blends.

- **Luberon AOP**
    - White, red, and rose wines; From a large complement of Rhone varietals.

- **Ventoux AOP**
    - White, red, and rose wines; From a large complement of Rhone varietals.

- **Côtes du Vivarais AOP**
    - White, red, and rose wines; From a large complement of Rhone varietals.

- **Costières de Nîmes AOP**
    - White, red. And rose wines; From a large complement of Rhone varietals.

- **Clairette de Bellegarde AOP**
    - White wines; Clairette grapes.

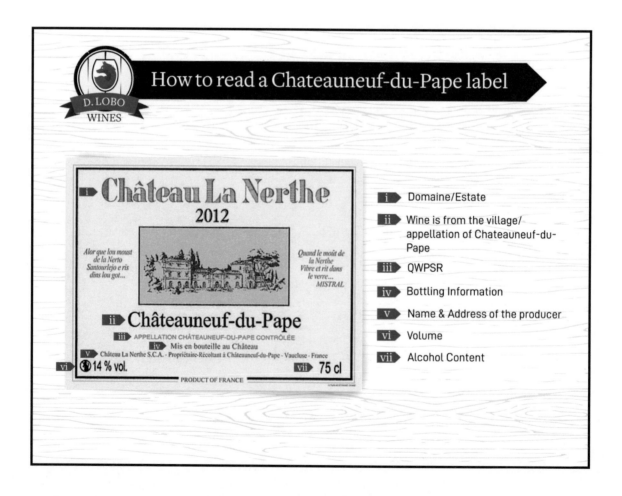

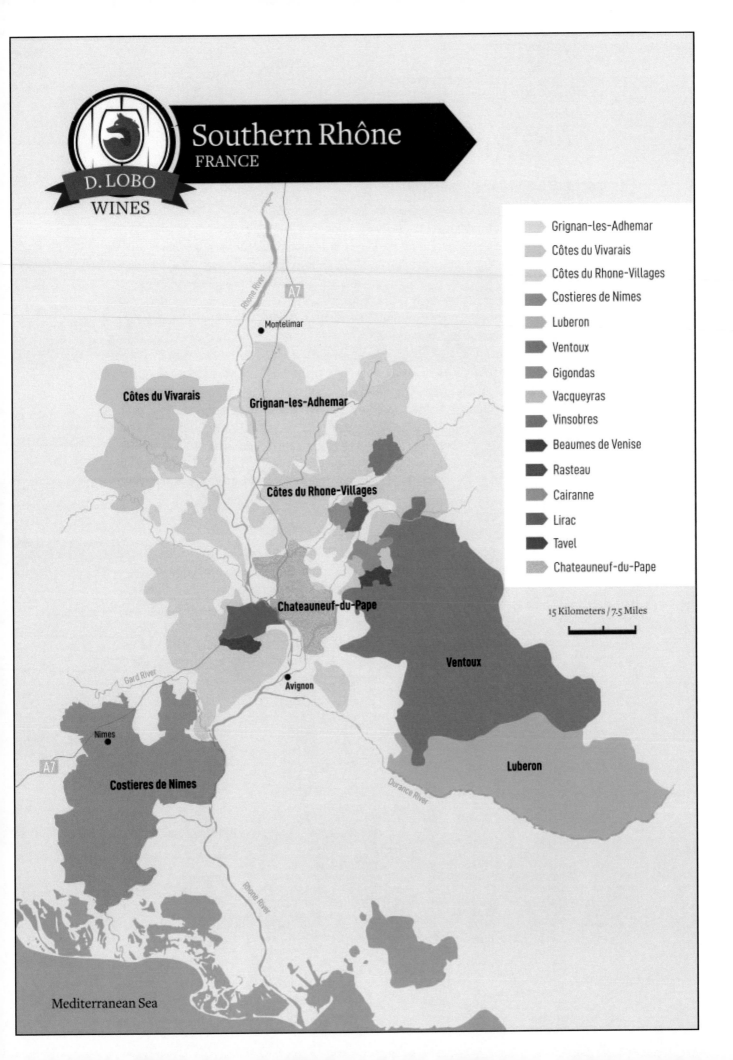

A GLANCE AT PROVENCE

Geographic and viticultural background

As every story starts somewhere, the story of wine begins in Provence. Located on the touristy Mediterranean coast, the sunny region is known for its herbs and gastronomy, as well as for its fresh translucid dry rosé wine and its Bandol AOP rouge.

Most of Provence's wines are labeled under Côtes de Provence AOP, an appellation that represents 90% blended rosé wines and only 10% reds and whites combined. Mainly sold in the region's traditional hourglass-shaped bottles (which is not to mistake with a guarantee of quality), Côtes de Provence AOP rosés must be made from at least two grape varieties, although it is important to note that blending of both white and red wines are not approved as method of production of still rosé. The label's darkest pink wines owe their color to the saignage method, the palest are made thanks to the immediate pressing of whole grapes. "And which varieties are used for the appellation's wines?", you ask. Well, Côte de Provence rouge and rosé blends are predominantly made from Cinsault, Grenache, Mourvèdre, Syrah and Tibouren grapes, some local to the region, some not. These two colors of wines can also be bottled under the Fréjus, La Londe, Notre-Dame des Anges, Pierrefeu and Saint-Victoire sub-appellations.

Now, as rosés are often associated with sun-drenched Provence, one rouge-dedicated appellation truly steals the spotlight... Indeed, Bandol AOP produces some of France's most intense reds and Provence's most valuable wines. Although Bandol also produces whites and rosés, its Mourvèdre-based rouge blends are a delectable asset to showcase on your table – Domaine Tempier and Château de Pibarnon are your best bets. The plummy grape accounts for at least 50% of Bandol reds and are often mixed with Cinsault and Grenache. The Carignan and Syrah also make some, but rare, apparitions in those wines. Described as plummy and animalistic, Bandol's red wines spend a minimum of 18 months in oak before their release, and producers tend to recommend opening the bottles only years after their sale for it to taste its best.

.

Unlike other wine regions in France, Provence does not need to worry about losing hurtful amounts of crops, as its dry and warm climate prevents mold and rot. The area's producers can even dare grow their vines organically, making their hard work sustainable but also incredibly valuable. For instance, winegrowers from Les Baux-de-Provence AOP have been trying to make this type of viticulture a standard - without concrete success, but it has not stopped them from working their organic magic. The appellation produces high quality Cinsault, Grenache and Syrah based reds and rosés, as well as Clairette, Grenache Blanc, Roussanne and Vermentino whites. Lying on top of a hill and protected from the vigorous Mistral – Les Baux-de-Provence hosts one of the best wine house of southern France, Domaine de Trevallon.

Other esteemed appellations of Provence include Bellet AOP, Cassis AOP, Côteaux-Varois-en-Provence AOP and Palette AOP, which all produce red, white and rosé wines. While Bellet is known for its quality Rolle (Vermentino) based white wines, Cassis uses the Clairette and Marsanne grapes for its best blancs. Contrastingly, Palette grows both red and white varieties and hosts one particularly good producer: Château Simone. Côteaux-Varois – which was first promoted as Vin de Pays before achieving AOP status in 1993 -, bottles quality wines of all three colors and is home to the excellent Domaine d'Triennes.

Along with Bordeaux, Côtes de Provence AOP is the only appellation in France to created a Grand Cru Classés ranking, with originally counted 23 domaines. This decision – coupled with the creation of new regulations and designations - has helped the region with maintaining high quality standards and further polish its reputation as fine wine region.

QUICK FACTS

Location and geography

Provence extends from the left bank of the lower Rhône to the west to the Italian border to the east, and is bordered by the Mediterranean Sea to the south.

Climate

The climate is dry and warm mediterranean.

Soil composition

The soil across Provence is a combination of many types. In isolated areas like Cassis and other vineyards near the Mediterranean coastline, limestone and shale dominate and make a perfect environment for white grapes. Other coastline areas in the region contain more schist and quartz in their composition, while inland vineyards tend to grow on clay and sandstone.

Vinification

While it helps cool the grapes and dry them after heavy rains (and therefore prevent rot and other diseases), the strong Mistral winds also bear negative effects, as it can also damage vines that are not securely trained and protected by hillsides. Where the wind is secifically dangerous, it is smarter to plant vineyards on hillsides facing south, towards the sea, using those slopes as a shield. In those areas, the type of grape varieties planted will also play a role since south-facing slopes receive the most sunshine and in the warm climate can easily over expose delicate and early ripening varieties which would be better suited on north-facing slopes.

Grape varieties

White

- Bourboulenc
- Clairette
- Grenache blanc
- Marsanne
- Viognier
- Chardonnay
- Sauvignon blanc
- Sémillon
- Rolle
- Ugni blanc

Red

- Mourvèdre
- Grenache
- Cinsault
- Cabernet Sauvignon
- Syrah
- Carignan
- Braquet
- Calitor
- Folle
- Tibouren

Some Provence producers

- **Châteaux la Rouvière**
- **Château Vannières**
- **Domaine de la Bégude**
- **Domaine de La Tour du Bon**
- **Domaine Tempier**

Provence appellations

- **Côtes de Provence AOP**
    - White, red, and rose wines. Rose accounts for nearly 90% of the appellation's output.

- **Bandol AOP**
    - White, red, and rose wines. A minimum 50% of the Mourvèdre grape is required.

- **Côteaux d'Aix-en-Provence AOP**
    - White, red, and roses wines.

- **Les Baux-de-Provence AOP**
    - White, red, and roses wines.

- **Cassis AOP**
    - White, red, and roses wines.

- **Palette AOP**
    - White, red, and roses wines.

- **Bellet AOP**
    - White, red, and roses wines.

- **Côteaux Varois en Provence AOP**
    - White, red, and roses wines.
    - ▸ Red wines; Grenache-based blends.

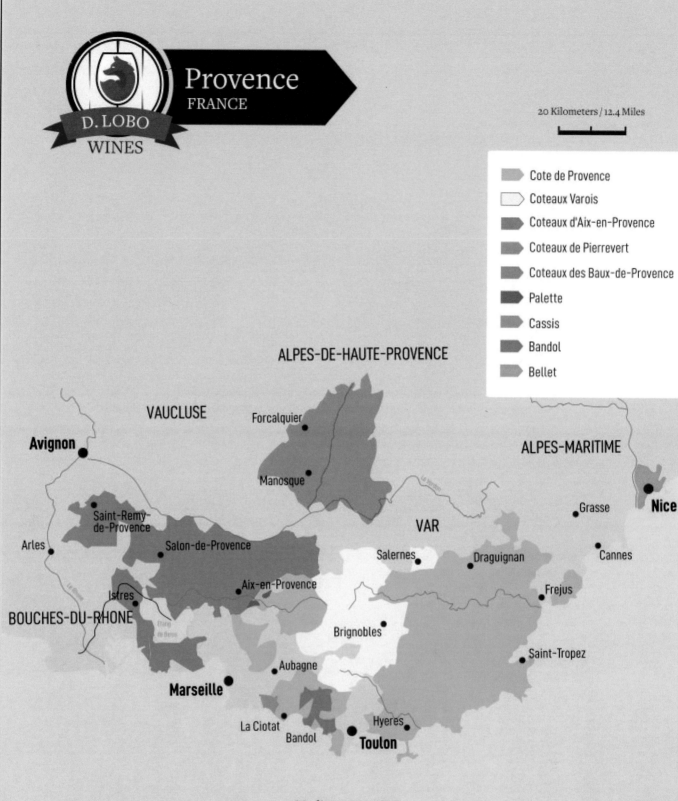

Provence
FRANCE

D. LOBO WINES

20 Kilometers / 12.4 Miles

Legend:
- Cote de Provence
- Coteaux Varois
- Coteaux d'Aix-en-Provence
- Coteaux de Pierrevert
- Coteaux des Baux-de-Provence
- Palette
- Cassis
- Bandol
- Bellet

ALPES-DE-HAUTE-PROVENCE

VAUCLUSE

Forcalquier

Avignon

ALPES-MARITIME

Nice

Manosque

Saint-Remy-de-Provence

Grasse

Arles

Salon-de-Provence

VAR

Cannes

Salernes

Draguignan

Aix-en-Provence

Frejus

Istres

BOUCHES-DU-RHONE

Etang de Berre

Brignobles

Saint-Tropez

Aubagne

Marseille

La Ciotat

Hyeres

Bandol

Toulon

Mediterranean Sea

A GLANCE AT CORSICA

Culturally independent from the rest of the country, Corsica and its warm, enveloping Mediterranean climate form one of Europe's most productive wine source. The plump, Italian sounding Nelluccio, Sciacarello and Vermentino grapes make some of the best wines in the country. Authentic to the island, those three varieties replaced some higher yielding but lower quality fruit like the Alicante Bouschet and Carignan.

Corsica's main appellation is Vin de Corse AOP and covers Nielluccio and Sciacarello-made rouge and rosés wines - often blended with Barbarossa and Grenache grapes – as well as Vermentino and Ugni Blanc whites. Borrowing its name from the island's capital city, Ajaccio AOP is one Corsica's two communal designation, Patrimonio AOP being the second. One last Coriscan appellation, Muscat du Cap Corse AOP, is known for its "vins doux naturels".

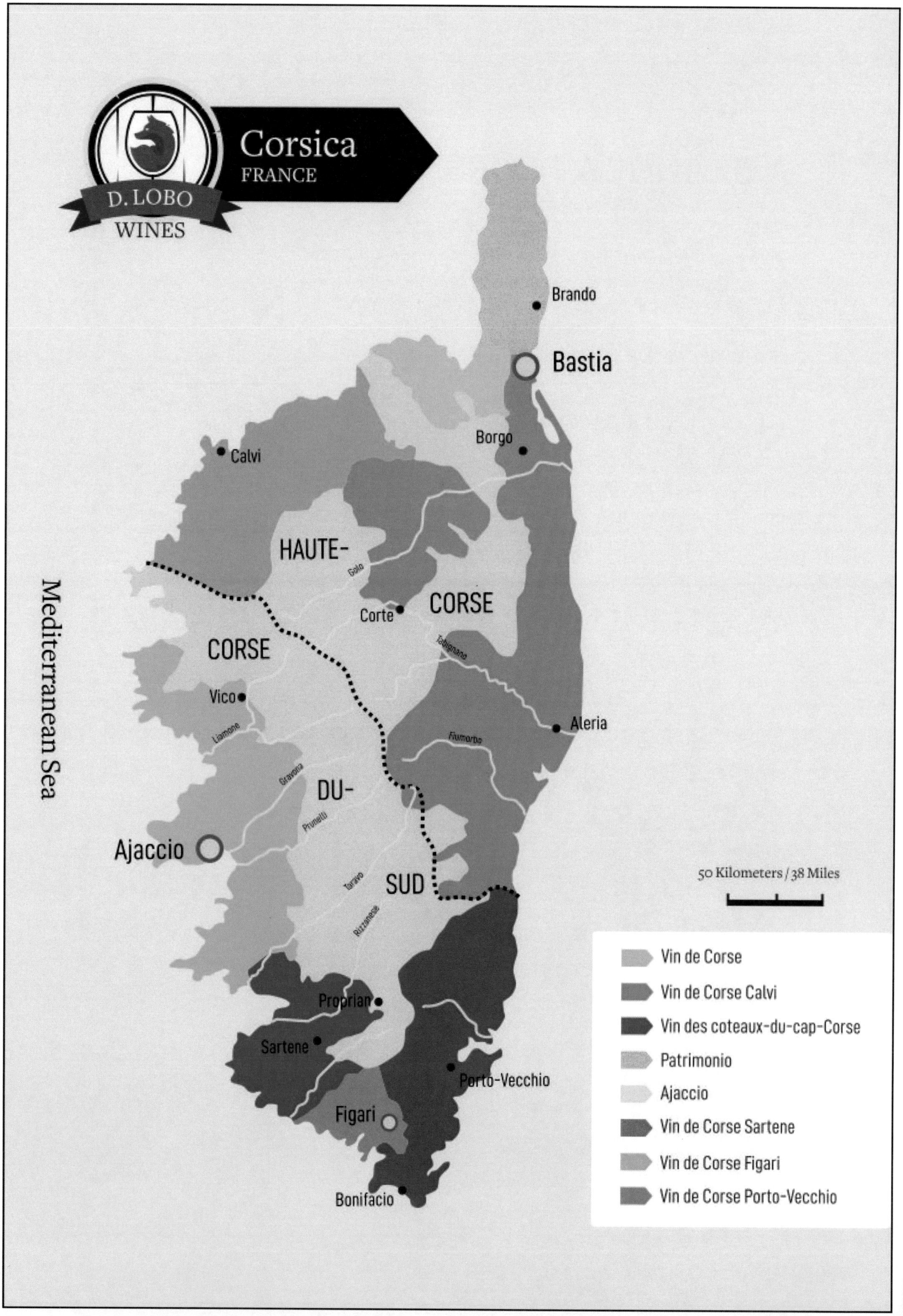

D. LOBO WINES

Corsica
FRANCE

Mediterranean Sea

Brando

Bastia

Calvi

Borgo

HAUTE-

Golo

Corte

CORSE

Tabignano

CORSE

Vico

Liamone

Aleria

Fiumorbo

Gravona

DU-

Prunelli

Ajaccio

Tavaro

SUD

Rizzanese

Proprian

Sartene

Porto-Vecchio

Figari

Bonifacio

50 Kilometers / 38 Miles

	Vin de Corse
	Vin de Corse Calvi
	Vin des coteaux-du-cap-Corse
	Patrimonio
	Ajaccio
	Vin de Corse Sartene
	Vin de Corse Figari
	Vin de Corse Porto-Vecchio

Location and geography

Corsica is located 11 km north of the island of Sardinia. It is a proud territorial collectivity of France. Many of the island's winemaking traditions and its grape varieties are of Italian origin.

Climate

Mediterranean, the climate is warmer and drier than in mainland France.

Soil composition

In the northern area of the Cap Corse peninsula, the soil is mainly composed of schist, and limestone and clay make up most of the Patrimonio's soils, just south of the Cap Corse. Along the island's west coast, granite dominates, and on the opposite coast, vineyards lie on a mix of marl and sand.

Grape varieties

White
- Vermentino
- Ugni Blanc

Red
- Carignan
- Alicante Bouschet
- Nielluccio (a variant of Sangiovese)
- Sciacarello
- Barbarossa

Corsica's regions and sub-regions

Today, Corsica has 9 AOP wine regions including the island-wide designation Vin de Corse AOP:

- **Patrimonio**
- **Ajaccio**

The generic Vin de Corse AOC covers the entire island and includes the smaller sub-regions of:

- **Vin de Corse-Côteaux du Cap Corse**
- **Vin de Corse-Calvi**
- **Vin de Corse-Figari**
- **Vin de Corse-Porto Vecchio**

- **Vin de Corse-Sartène**
- **Vin de Corse AOC**
- **Muscat du Cap Corse AOC**

Includes the vin doux naturel wines.

A GLANCE AT LANGUEDOC-ROUSSILLON

Languedoc

The warm wine region of Languedoc-Roussillon proudly stands in the shape of crescent on the southern coast of France. The region's climate allows for vineyards to grow lush and sweet, which helped Languedoc-Roussillon to collectively become the largest vine acreage in the world. As France produced about 56 million hectoliters of wine in 2006, the region contributed

up to 30% of this number, with a whopping 16 million hectoliters. A lot of Languedoc-Roussillon's production, however, display lower quality traits, and although the area does not grow nearly as much vines (since many plantings only qualify for the generic Vin de France appellation), it still largely contributes to Europe's market surplus.

One of the region's oldest appellations, Fitou AOP, is actually not as ancient as others in the country, since it was only inaugurated in 1948. Nonetheless, the western-Languedoc appellation provides quality Carignan-based reds. Divided in two zones, Fitou Maritime (Marine Fitou) and Fitou Montagneux (Mountainous Fitou), the AOP lies within the larger Corbières AOP - which crafts reds, rosés, and a few white wines. Corbières benefits from an eclectic soil composition and varied microclimates. Minervois AOP, located to the north of Corbières, also produces all three colors of wines and is split into several areas with one in particular, the rouge dedicated Minervois-La-Livinière, that achieved AOP status in 1999. More versatile, the Faugères and Saint-Chinian AOPs provide reds, whites and rosés from grapes that may sprout all over the South of France. Saint-Chinian, along with its Berlou and Roquebrun areas, started producing white wines only recently.

For reds and rosés only, you will want to head to the Cabardes and Malepère AOPs. As the first one presses Grenache, Syrah and red Bordeaux grapes for its wines, the second makes its rouge from a minimum of 50% Merlot and its rosé with a composition of half Cabernet Franc. Right under the Cabardes and Malepère duo, Limoux AOP offers Merlot-based reds as well as Chardonnay, Chenin Blanc and local Mauzac still whites that must complete their fermentation in oak barrels. The ancient, méthode traditionnelle Blanquette de Limoux bubbly wine is made from 90% Mauzac, and the more modern Crémant de Limoux contains no more than 20% of the grape, making room for favored Chardonnay and Chenin Blanc.

To the east of the aforementioned appellations lies the regional and dominant Languedoc AOP, formerly known as Côteaux du Languedoc AOC. Languedoc AOP labels reds, rosés and whites produced from a total of 11 geographic designations all over Languedoc-Roussillon. The AOP's reds generally comprise a 50% blend of Grenache, Mourvèdre, Lladoner Pelut and Mourvèdre.

A Languedoc grand cru system has yet to be established in the region, although it would help clarify the region's quality standards and boost its best wines on every market. For now, some crus and geographical designations successively get promoted to AOP status. Terrasses du Larzac, in 2014, and La Clape, the following year, both were lucky enough to achieve independent AOP designations.

Before wrapping these paragraphs about the beautiful Languedoc, let's not forget about its fortified wine AOPs, like Muscat de Frontignan, Muscat de Mireval, Muscat de Lunel and Muscat de Saint-Jean-de-Minervois. The most famous wines, coming from Muscat de Frontignan, are labeledas vin doux naturel or vin de liqueur.

Location and geography

Situated in the South of France, the region of Languedoc runs northward along the Mediterranean coast from the border with Spain.

Climate

The climate is mediterranean. Summers are hot and dry, and spring and autumn are also fairly warm with a few frosty mornings in April. Winters are also pretty mild and luckily sunny as temperatures rarely reach below 0°C.

Soil composition

The region's soils are very fairly diverse, with chalk, limestone and gravel inland, and alluvial soils near the coast.

Grape varieties

White
- Chardonnay
- Chenin Blanc
- Mauzac

Red
- Carignan
- Grenache
- Cinsault
- Syrah
- Mourvèdre
- Cabernet Sauvignon
- Cabernet Franc
- Merlot
- Malbec
- Petit Verdot
- Pinot Noir
- Lledoner Pelut

Languedoc appellations

- Fitou AOP
- Divided into two distinct, noncontiguous sectors: Fitou Maritime and Fitou Montagneux.
▸ The wines are red blends, usually dominated by Carignan.

- Corbières AOP
- White, red and rosé wines.
▸ One subzone, Corbières-Boutenac, has achieved full appellation status for Carignan-based red wines.

- Minervois AOP
- White, red and rosé wines.
▸ Divided into several distinct subzones. The center of the appellation, Minervois-La Livinière, received its own appellation in 1999 for red wines.

- Cabardes AOP
- Red and rosé wines.

- Malepère AOP
- Red and rosé wines.

- Saint-Chinian AOP
- White, red and rosé wines.

- Faugères AOP
- White, red and rosé wines.

- Limoux AOP
- White and red wines, and sparkling wines.

- Crémant de Limoux AOP
- Maximum 20% Mauzac and Pinot Noir in favor of Chardonnay and Chenin Blanc.
▸ Tiny quantities of Limoux méthode ancestrale are made solely from Mauzac, wherein the wine's fermentation arrests in the cold of winter, reawakening in the spring.

- Languedoc AOP (Formerly Côteaux de Languedoc AOP)
- White, red and rosé wines.

- **Muscat de Mireval AOP**
    - Fortified wines.

- **Muscat de Lunel AOP**
    - Fortified wines.

- **Muscat de Saint-Jean-de-Minervois AOP**
    - Fortified wines.

- **Muscat de Frontignan AOP**
    - Muscat de Frontignan wines are most common and may be either vin doux naturel or vin de liqueur.

The Languedoc-Roussillon might be the best-kept wine secret in France

- **Château l'Hospitalet, Narbonne**
- **Domaine Riberach, Bélesta**
- **La Maison Noilly Prat**
- **Les Clos de Paulilles**
- **Port-Vendres**
- **Domaine Royal de Jarras**
- **Aigues-Mortes**
- **Abbaye de Valmagne**

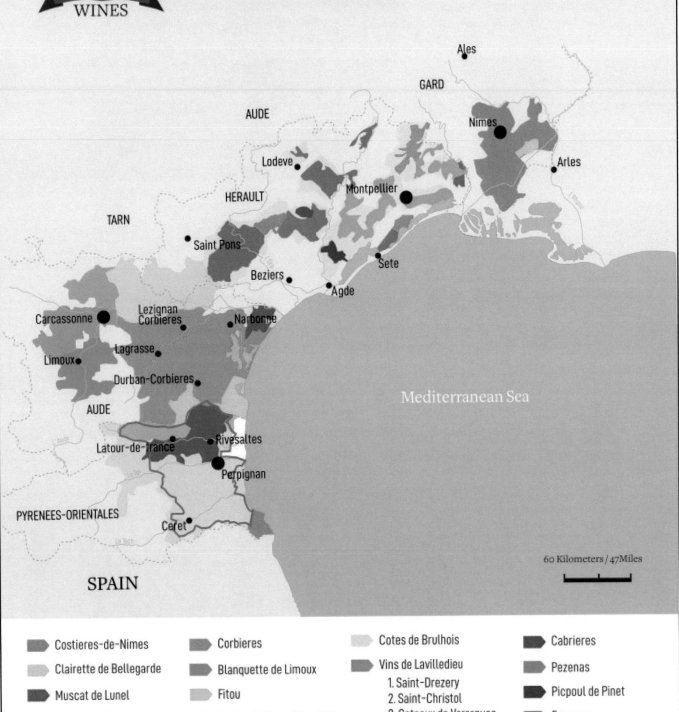

Langedoc-Roussillon
FRANCE

D. LOBO
WINES

Ales

GARD

AUDE

Nimes

Lodeve

Arles

Montpellier

HERAULT

TARN

Saint Pons

Sete

Beziers

Agde

Lezignan
Corbieres

Carcassonne

Narborne

Lagrasse

Limoux

Durban-Corbieres

Mediterranean Sea

AUDE

Latour-de-france

Rivesaltes

PYRENEES-ORIENTALES

Perpignan

Ceret

60 Kilometers / 47Miles

SPAIN

Costieres-de-Nimes	Corbieres	Cotes de Brulhois	Cabrieres
Clairette de Bellegarde	Blanquette de Limoux	Vins de Lavilledieu	Pezenas
Muscat de Lunel	Fitou	1. Saint-Drezery	Picpoul de Pinet
Muscat de Mireval	Cotes-de-Roussillon-Villages	2. Saint-Christol	Faugeres
Muscat de Frontignan	Maury	3. Coteaux de Verargues	Saint-Chinian
Muscat de Saint-Jean-de-Minervois	Cotes-du-Roussillon	4. Coteaux de la Mejanelle	La Clape
Cotes de Duras	Collioure, Banyuls	5. Saint-Georges d'Orques	Quatourze
Cotes du Marmandais	— Riversaltes	Pic-Saint-Loup	
		Terrasses du Larzac	
		1. Saint-Saturnin	
		2. Montpeyroux	

Roussillon

The Roussillon region lies and rises right above the Spanish border, and is specifically known for its vin doux naturel as over 90% of the country's fortified wines are crafted there. Rivesaltes AOP – which means "high reverbanks" in Catalan - is the only appellation for these sweet, varietal or blended wines and actually is the birthplace of vin doux naturel. It was physician Arnaud de Villeneuve who introduced the mutage method in the region, for medicinal purposes at first. The label covers an impressive array of fortified vin doux naturel styles, such as

ambre, grenat, rosé and tuile (amber, red, pink and tawny). Ambre and tuile wines are oxidated until March 1 of the 3rd year following the harvest – although producers often extend aging for these wines -, while Grenats are bottled before June 30 of the 2nd year. Oxidative wines are either aged under the sun and in glass bonbonnes (demijohn) or through the solera method. The Rivesaltes wines that are aged for at least 5 years are known under "hors d'âge" wines and may sometimes be released only after 20 years of aging!

Rivesaltes' Mediterranean vineyards grow Grenache Blanc, Gris and Noir, Maccabeo, Muscat d'Alexandrie, Muscat à Petits Grains and Tourbat. Grenache Noir accounts for 100% of grenat wines and can be blended with white varieties to produce tuiles. The same grape is used for at least 50% of Banyuls AOP traditional fortified wines. Understandably, Banyuls Grand Cru bottles require a minimum of 75% Grenache Noir and must spend 30 months or more in barrel. The appellation's wines are some of France's most full-bodied and intense wines. Banyuls' unfortified red, white and rosés are generally released as Collioure AOP. Maury AOP also uses Grenache Noir for its wines, but also allows the Blanc and Gris varieties. Unlike Banyul's, the designation's vignerons can release their dry red wines under the Maury AOP as well, since 2011. Lastly, If only Muscat is used for a wine, then it can be labeled the namesake Muscat de Rivesaltes AOP. The sub-appellation's sweeter wines are generally released earlier and are therefore meant for youthful consumption.

The dry red, white and rosé appellation of Côtes du Roussillon AOP covers 32 communes, located to the north of Les Aspres. The Côtes du Roussillon Les Aspres sub-area is notable for its Syrah production as well as for the Mourvèdre reds of the Albères Mountains and of Les Aspres. Four villages, Caramany, Latour-de-France, Lesquerde and Tautavel, are allowed to append their names Côtes du Roussillon AOP.

Although vins doux naturels are emblematic to Roussillon's wine production, some of the region's vignerons are rediscovering the potential of old plantings and are now crafting more styles of esteemed quality wines...

Location and geography

Roussillon is situated in the South of France, running northward along the Mediterranean coast from the border with Spain.

Climate

The climate is mediterranean. Summers are hot and dry with spring and autumn being rather warm, despite a few possible frosty mornings in April. Winters are also quite mild and sunny with temperatures rarely falling below 0°C.

Soil composition

Varies from the chalk, limestone and gravel based soils inland to more alluvial soils near the coast.

Grape varieties

White
- Chardonnay
- Chenin Blanc
- Mauzac

Red
- Carignan
- Grenache
- Cinsault
- Syrah
- Mourvèdre
- Cabernet Sauvignon
- Cabernet Franc
- Merlot
- Malbec
- Petit Verdot
- Pinot Noir
- Lledoner Pelut

Some Roussillon producers

- **Château d'Oupia**
- **Château Saint-Roch**
- **Domaine de l'Hortus**
- **Domaine d'Aupilhac**

Roussillon appellations

- Rivesaltes AOP
- Wines aged for a minimum of 5 years may be called hors d'âge; in practice these may receive up to 20 years of aging prior to release.
▸ The fortified wines of Rivesaltes may be varietal wines or blends.
- Grenache (Noir, Gris, and Blanc), Maccabeo, Tourbat, Muscat of Alexandria, and Muscat a Petits Grains. While Grenache Noir is the sole component of grenat wines, producers of tuile styles may blend the grape with white varieties.

- Muscat de Rivesaltes AOP
- Wine produced solely from the two Muscat varieties.

- Maury AOP
- Vin doux naturel.
▸ Grenache Noir, Blanc, Gris.

- Banyuls AOP
- Grenache Noir accounts for at least 50% of the Traditionnel fortified reds.

- Banyuls Grand Cru AOP
- Requires at least 75%. To be labeled grand cru, Banyuls must spend a minimum 30 months in barrel. If destined to be vintage-dated, Banyuls is generally bottled within one year and labeled rimage.

- Collioure AOP
- Unfortified red, white, and rose wines from the producers of Banyuls are released as Collioure AOPs.

- Côtes du Roussillon AOP
- White, red, and a high percentage of rose wines. A subzone, Côtes du Roussillon Les Aspres, was recognized in 2003 for Syrah and Mourvèdre-based red wines from the villages nestled within the area of Les Aspres and the Albères Mountains.

- Côtes du Roussillon-Villages AOP
- Red wines of 32 communes to the north of Les Aspres. Four communes may add their names to the appellation: Latour-de-France, Caramany, Lesquerde, and Tautavel. As ambitious producers discover a wealth of old vine plantings, trim yields, and rethink the worth of once-derided workhorse grapes like Carignan, Roussillon's reputation for wines beyond the traditional vins doux naturel will continue to rise.
- Fortified wines.

A GLANCE AT THE SUD-OUEST

Southwestern France and the Dordogne

The wines of the Sud-Ouest (Southwestern France)'s vineyards resemble those of Bordeaux and of the Sud-Est (Southeastern France), as well as those of Spain. For instance, some AOP's like the beautiful region of Bergerac, produce all three types of wines from Bordeaux grapes. Pecharmant AOP blended reds are the longest-lived wines of Bergerac, and Côtes de Montravel AOP, Haut-Montravel AOP, Monbazillac AOP, Saussignac AOP and Rosette AOP make some of Bergerac's sweetest whites. The esteemed Monbazillac is notably known for crafting botrytised wines from Bordeaux varietals. The designation's sandy soils are especially a great source of nutrients for Muscadelle, and the ban on mechanical harvesting make Monbazillac one of the best-quality producers in the Sud-Ouest. Bergerac and its sub-AOP also form a beautiful region with the Dordogne river flowing right through it, from the Massif Central mountains to the Gironde estuary.

South of Bordeaux, Cahors AOP, Gaillac AOP, Jurancon AOP and Madiran AOP all make a diverse and quality selection of wines. The first one, located on the Lot river, produces rustic reds mainly made from Malbec (at least 70%) but allowing Tannat and Merlot. Gaillac AOP, on the other hand, crafts wines of all three colors. The appellation actually one of France's oldest vineyards, as they were first inaugurated by Romans in the 1st century. For its reds, Gaillac mostly uses Duras, Fer, Gamay and Syrah grapes, sometimes allowing red Bordeaux varieties to its blends. For its whites, Mauzac, Muscadelle and Len de l'El are the only ones that made the cut. The latter variety means "far from sight" in the old d'Oc language, and depicts the clusters distance to the eye, or bud, from which they grow. Len de l'El is responsible for soft and "gulpable" textures that perfectly balance out the Mauzac grape's acidity. The AOP's sweet whites are designated as Gaillac Doux, and the sparkling ones are sold under Gaillac Mousseux, which can be made by méthode traditionnelle or méthode Gaillacoise – a method that actually comes from the méthode ancestrale. A specific appellation, Première Côtes, was created to label the dry "sec" white wines of Gaillac's 11 delimited communes.

Next are the Gros and Petit Manseng white wines of Jurancon, produced in the Pyrénées-Atlantiques department. While the Gros Manseng variety is used for Jurancon Sec AOP's tangy dry whites, the Petit Manseng is chosen for sweet passerillage bottles.

167

The Camaralet, Lauzet and Petit Courbu grapes may be used as secondary grapes for both Jurancon dry and sweet wines.

As for Madiran AOP, the appellation provides an intense, tannic rouge principally made from Tannat, and allowing Cabernet Franc, Cabernet Sauvignon and Fer as secondary varieties. Madiran wines were originally so acidic that a local winemaker, Patrick Ducournau, thought of a way to soften the region's production and came up with a micro-oxygenation technique in the 1990s. Some of the region's producers also craft Arrufiac, Petit Courbu and Petit Manseng sweet and semi-sweet whites under the Pacherenc du Vic-Bilh AOP.

Lastly, we cannot forget to mention the unique Marcillac AOP designation, which produces reds made from a required minimum of 90% Fer. Some other appellations, like Buzet AOP, Côtes de Duras AOP and Côtes de Marmandais AOP, are notable for their Bordeaux like wines, the latter allowing regional varieties like Syrah to its blends. The Fronton AOP label, on the other hand, likes to mainly used grapes from the area, and actually produces blended reds and rosés with a minimum 40% Négrette.

Some of the Sud-Ouest Vin Délimité de Qualité Supérieure vineyards achieved AOP status fairly recently, in the end of 2011.

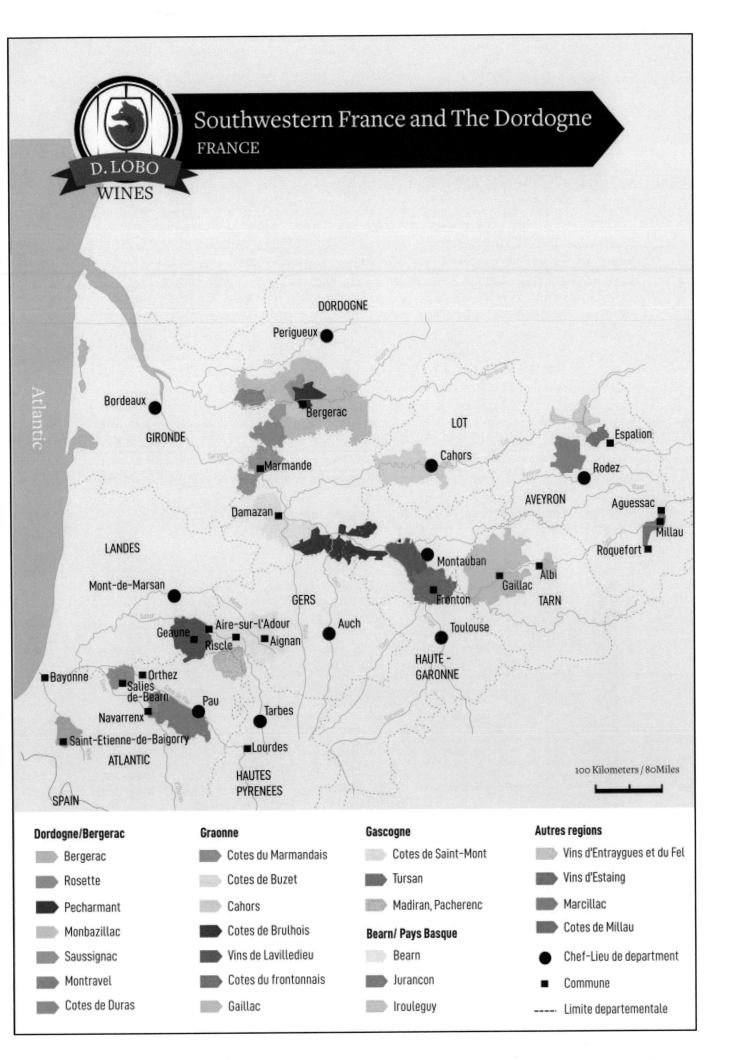

Sud-Ouest (Southwestern France)

Like in Burgundy, viticulture was brought in the Sud-Ouest (also known as the High Country) by the wine-loving Romans, and the region was even an active part of wine trading long before Bordeaux's first vineyards were planted. When Bordeaux finally became the harbor city it is now, southwestern bottles would be shipped there via the Dordogne and Garonne's affluent streams. However, the region's trade started getting highly regulated when the négociants of Bordeaux accused southwestern wines of threatening their economic interest...

In fact, the inland High Country holds a clear climatic advantage over Bordeaux, as its weather displays warmer temperatures that allow earlier harvests and stronger alcohol levels. Around the 1300s were inaugurated the "police des vins", which dropped some restrictions on the use of the port of Bordeaux specifically for wine trading. The authority group made it so that no wine could travel out of Bordeaux until most of the area's wines had been sold. Needless to say, these rules put a real strain on the Sud-Ouest's wine industry: the region's barrels would be kept in Bordeaux warehouses for weeks, sometimes months before being sold for much cheaper than their true value! By the time southwestern bottles would be put on the market, the latter had already been overcrowded.

Château Malartrie

Location and geography

Known as "France's Hidden Corner", the Sud-Ouest (or South West) hides between the Pyrénées Mountains, Spain, Bordeaux and the Atlantic Ocean.

The region is divided into four "sub-regions" that each owns its distinctive character, climate, and grapes:

- Bergerac & Dordogne River
- Garonne & Tarn
- Lot River
- Pyrénées

These four areas all boast renowned village appellations or AOPs that adhere to strict viticulture and production regulations.

Some larger areas, with less restrictive winemaking regulations, bear the IGP label, which stands for "Indications Géographique Protégée", or Protected Geographical Indication. You can see how they are laid out on the South West France wine map.

Climate

The region's climate is overall Mediterranean, although each sub-region displays its own microclimates.

Soil composition

The soils range from sand, clay, and gravel in most parts of the region. The stone type of soil, is however, found in the plateau areas and on base areas of Pyrénées.

BERGERAC AND DORDOGNE RIVER

Location and geography

Bergerac and the Dordogne river are located just south of Bordeaux, the vineyards of the 80 communes of this region lie along the Dordogne River.

Climate

The climate is Mediterranean. The Dordogne River and the Atlantic Ocean tend to influence the region's climate, although temperatures are slightly higher than in other regions.

Soil composition

The soils of Bergerac are fairly diverse, as limestone from ancient marine deposits and boulbènes soils can be found in the region. Clay and limestone forma great environment for the development of structured and aromatic grapes.

Grape varieties

White
- Sauvignon Blanc
- Ugni Blanc
- Sémillon
- Chenin Blanc
- Muscadelle
- Ondenc

Red
- Cabernet Sauvignon
- Cabernet Franc
- Merlot
- Malbec (called Cot)
- Mérille

Vinification

Producers use similar grape varieties to make dry red, white, rose and sweet dessert styles.

Bergerac and Dordogne sub-appellations

- **Bergerac AOP**
  - White, red, and rose wines, single variety, and blends.

- **Côtes de Duras AOP**
  - White and red wines.

- **Côtes de Montravel AOP**
  - Sweet wines.

- **Haut-Montravel AOP**
  - Sweet wines.

- **Monbazillac AOP**
  - Sweet wines.

- **Montravel AOP**
  - White and red dry wines.

- **Pécharmant AOP**
  - Red blends.

- **Rosette AOP**
  - Sweet wines.

- **Saussignac AOP**
  - Sweet wines.

GARONNE AND TARN

Location and geography

The region of Tarn and the Garonne River are located further east, towards the city of Toulouse.

Climate

As the west of the area gets climatic influences from the Atlantic, the east gets the Mediterranean seas's warmth and fewer rain falls.

Soil composition

The region's soils are composed of clay, gravel terraces, limestone and boulbènes.

Grape varieties

White
- White Wines
- Len de L'El
- Mauzac Blanc
- Mauzac Rose
- Saint Côme (Rousselou)
- Sauvignon Blanc
- Ugni Blanc
- Sémillon
- Chenin Blanc
- Muscadelle
- Ondenc

Red
- Fer Servadou (native to the Basque region of Spain)
- Duras
- Gamay
- Négrette
- Syrah
- Tannat
- Abouriou
- Prunelard (ancient native variety and father of Malbec)
- Cinsault
- Jurançon Noir
- Mouyssaguese
- Pinot Noir
- Mérille

Garonne and Tarn sub-appellations

- **Brulhois AOC**
  - Red and rose wines.

- **Buzet AOC**
  - White, red, and rose wines.

- **Cahors AOC**
  - Reds made predominantly from Malbec with small quantities of Tannat and Merlot.

- **Côtes de Duras AOC**
  - White, red, and rose wines.

- **Côtes du Marmandais AOC**
  - White, red, and rose wines.

- **Fronton AOC**
  - Red and rose wines. Négrette must account for at least 40% of the blend of any wine.

- **Gaillac AOC**
  - White, red, and sparkling wines.

- **Marcillac AOC**
  - Red wines predominantly from Fer Servadou.

- **Côteaux du Quercy VDQS**
  - Red wines predominantly Cabernet Franc.

- **Côtes de Millau VDQS**
  - Red based Gamay ans Syrah wines, also some white and rose wines.

- **Saint-Sardos VDQS**
  - Red, and rose wines, predominantly from Syrah and Tannat.

- **Vins de Lavilledieu VDQS**
  - Red and rose wines.

- **Vins d'Entraygues et du Fel VDQS**
  - White, red, and rose wines.

- **Vins d'Estaing VDQS**
  - White, red, and rose wines. Chenin Blanc, Fer, and Gamay.

LOT RIVER

Location and geography

Southeast of Bordeaux, the Lot department lies on the southern border of the Massif Central mountain range, which occupies a significant part of the territory in southeast France.

Climate

As the west of the area gets climatic influences from the Atlantic, the east gets the Mediterranean seas's warmth and fewer rain falls.

Soil composition

The region's soils are composed of clay, gravel terraces, limestone and boulbènes.

Grape varieties

White
- White Wines
- Len de L'El
- Mauzac Blanc
- Mauzac Rose
- Saint Côme (Rousselou)
- Sauvignon Blanc
- Ugni Blanc
- Sémillon
- Chenin Blanc
- Muscadelle
- Ondenc

Red
- Fer Servadou (native to the Basque region of Spain)
- Duras
- Gamay
- Négrette
- Syrah
- Tannat
- Abouriou
- Prunelard (ancient native variety and father of Malbec)
- Cinsault
- Jurançon Noir
- Mouyssaguese
- Pinot Noir
- Mérille

PYRÉNÉES

Location and geography

Located in southwest Europe, the Pyrénées mountain range forms a beautiful and natural border between Spain and France.

Climate

The climate there is overall Mediterranean, much drier than the coastal areas to the south with burning heat during the day and cooler evenings. Some areas are deemed more Maritime.

Soil composition

Sandstone and quartz are found in the foothills, as well as sandy clays and loams.

Grape varieties

White
- Chardonnay
- Camaralet
- Gros Manseng
- Petit Manseng
- Lauzet
- Arrufiac
- Raffiat
- Courbu
- Clairette Blanche
- Baroque

- And other grape varieties from close by.

Red
- Syrah
- Pinot Noir
- Manseng Noir
- Tannat
- Courbu Noir
- Fer Servadou

- And the Bordeaux grape varieties.
- Other grape varieties from close by.

Vinification

Pyrénées is known for its cool-climate styles of Shiraz, as well as sparkling wines made in the traditional style from Pinot Noir and Chardonnay. All three colors of wine are produced.

Pyrénées appellations

- **Madiran AOP**
    - Red wine only, predominantly Tannat winesRed and rose wines.

- **Pacherenc du Vic Bilh AOP**
    - Sweet late-harvest dessert blended wines.

- **Irouléguy AOP**
    - White and red wines, predominantly Cabernet Franc, Tannat, and white blends..

- **Tursan AOP**
    - White wines from the Baroque native grape. Red wines predominantly from Cabernet Franc and Tannat.

- **Saint-Mont AOP**
    - Red and rose wines predominantly from cabernet Franc, Tannat, and Fer Servadou.

- **Béarn AOP**
    - White, red, and rose wines.

- **Jurançon AOP**
    - White wines only, dry and sweet.
    - ►The fortified wines of Rivesaltes may be varietal wines or blends.
    - Grenache (Noir, Gris, and Blanc), Maccabeo, Tourbat, Muscat of Alexandria, and Muscat a Petits Grains. While Grenache Noir is the sole component of grenat wines, producers of tuile styles may blend the grape with white varieties.

GRAPE GLOSSARY

Altesse

Offers complex aromas, ranging from rose to apricot kernel and tropical fruits, together with pepper and sweet spices. Dried fruits and honey hints also appear when there's noble rot. Simple Altesse wines with no specific origin beyond AC Alsace are usually medium bodied and either off-dry or semi-sweet.

Cabernet Franc

Cabernet Franc is a classic and delicate, medium-bodied rouge showing moderate tannins and balancing out fruity aromas such as cherry, raspberry, strawberry and tomato with peppery and herbal notes.

Chasselas

The Chasselas grape can be complex and rich, showing a range of fruity, floral, and minerals flavors, with good acidity and ability to age. Fruit like red apple, apple blossom, melon, best describe the character of this white wine grape, with notes of mint and smoke.

Gewurztraminer

Like the Altesse grape, the Gewurztraminer variety offers rich tropical, flowery and spicy aromas. Dried fruits and honey hints also appear when there's noble rot. Simple Gewurz wines with no specific origin beyond AC Alsace are usually medium bodied and either off-dry or semi-sweet.

Gringet

Especially when oak-aged, the wine can take on a creamy, textured mouthfeel. Pinot blanc often exhibits notes of citrus, pear, apple, and occasional smoke or mineral undertones. The nose is almond, light spice, and sometimes fruitiness. Unoaked pinot blanc is low in tannins.

Grolleau

Indigenous to the Loire Valle, the Grolleau grape produces light bodied rosé wines with high acidity. It is often produced in off-dry to medium sweet style, leaving residual suger in the wine to balance out the sourness.

Gros Plant

Fruity and floral, Gros Plant is light to the taste and shows an elegant brightness and vibrant fruity notes. Wines made from this grape and aged on lees gain a rounder and gulpable result. Lees aging also give Gros Plant du Pays Nantais wines crisp and direct textures.

Jacquère

Intense aromas that rise from the glass (even when the wine is ice cold). This aromatic wine offers primary fruit aromas of orchard fruits like nectarine, apricot, honey-crisp apple, and pear.

Melon de Bourgogne

With its natural high acidity, Melon de Bourgogne add apple, citrus flavors and soft, latent mineral notes to any wine. The grape also tends to show a slight saltiness, translating the region's Mediterranean breeze.

Mondeuse

Takes on a different character. These wines often show richer, with honey and melon notes.

Muscat

Wines are characterized by a fresh, fruit grapy character where you will find some white pepper, grape seed, roses, mint (from the Muscat a petits grains) and, most obviously, the aroma of freshly crushed grapes.

Orbois

The Orbois grape aromas include lemon balm, hazelnuts, almonds and occasionally a hint of vanilla and liquorice. Roses have red berry aroma. Elegant on the palate, fresh, sometimes crisp and lively, while demi secs are more gentle, roses can be slightly tannic.

Persan

Similar to the Mondeuse, the Persan variety display specific and makes rich wines with honey and melon notes.

Pineau d'Anis

In red wine, the grape brings a slightly tannic taste. In all three colors, it shows noticeable acidity and white pepper notes.

Pinot Blanc

Like the Gringet grape, Pinot Blanc, especially when oak-aged, offers a creamy, textured mouthfeel to its wines. Pinot blanc often exhibits notes of citrus, pear, apple, and occasional smoke or mineral undertones. The nose is almond, light spice, and sometimes fruitiness. Unoaked pinot blanc is low in tannins.

Pinot Gris

Flavors and aromas vary greatly from region to region and from style to style. But common features include notes of pears, apples, stonefruit, tropical fruit, sweet spices and even a hint of smoke or wet wool.

Poulsard

Wines made from this grape are refreshing and display cherry, leafy notes.

Riesling

Similar to the Jacquère grape, the Riesling offers intense aromas that rise from the glass (even when the wine is ice cold), with predominant fruity hints of orchard like nectarine, apricot, honey-crisp apple, and pear.

Romorantin

The Romorantin grape has a light nose of pear, lemon peel and pineapple. The white wine created from the grapes is acidic with intense minerality and fruit. Tasting notes include stewed apples, lemon and honey.

Roussanne

Similar to Muscat bottlings, Roussanne wines are characterized by a fresh, fruit grapy character where you will find some white pepper, grape seed, roses, mint (from the Muscat a petits grains) and, most obviously, the aroma of freshly crushed grapes.

Savagnin

Refreshing and elegant, Savagnin displays floral and citrus aromas. It can be thought as Sauvignon Blanc without the grassy notes, or as a non-oaked Chardonnay.

Sylvaner

Like its Mondeuse and Persan cousins, the Sylvaner grape takes on a different, richer character than most, and offer honey and melon notes.

Trousseau

Displaying deep cherry colored wines, Trousseau makes wines high in alcohol and in candy-like sourness. Their taste is a perfect balance between red berries and mossy minerals.